HANNAH HURNARD
The Authorized Biography

Hannah Hurnard

THE AUTHORIZED BIOGRAPHY

The Story behind the Spiritual Classic
Hind's Feet on High Places

John Wood

Monarch
Olive Press
Struik Christian Books

First published 1996

ISBN 1 85424 334 9

British Library Cataloguing in Publication Data.
A catalogue record for this book is available
from the British Library.

Co-published with:
Olive Press, The Church's Ministry among Jewish people
30c Clarence Road, St Albans, Herts AL1 4JJ

Struik Christian Books Ltd.
Cornelis Struik House, 80 McKenzie Street
Cape Town 8001, South Africa
Reg no 04/2203/06

Production and Printing in England for
MONARCH PUBLICATIONS
Broadway House, The Broadway, Crowborough,
East Sussex TN6 1HQ
by Nuprint Ltd, Station Road, Harpenden, Herts, AL5 4SE

*Dedicated with much esteem
to Marjorie Hurnard:
living link with Hannah,
whose story she shared.*

Contents

Foreword 9

1. Ginger Beer and Poetry 11
2. A Quaker Homestead 17
3. Little Miss Much-Afraid 25
4. Damaged Reed and Smouldering Wick 34
5. Warfare Ended: Sin Forgiven 40
6. In the Service of the Shepherd 47
7. Those Two Veiled Guides 54
8. A Stop-gap in Haifa 61
9. Detour through the Desert 69
10. The Valley of Buds and Fruits 76
11. A Baby Austin Motor Car 83
12. Paper Time Bombs 90
13. Across the Divide 96
14. Highways and Byways 103
15. A Blue Morris Van 111
16. End of an Era 119
17. Keswick 1951 126
18. Intercessors for Israel 136
19. The Making of Books 143
20. Closing the Door behind Her 150
21. To the Law and the Testimony 160
22. Hannah's Legacy 166

Acknowledged with Gratitude 177
Landmarks in Hannah's Story 181
From the Hurnard Family Tree 184
The Judgment of the Cross by Rose Hurnard 186

Foreword

To many hosts of people around the world, Hannah Hurnard's famous book *Hinds' Feet on High Places*, has been quite literally a Godsend. Even now, more than forty years after the book was first published, it remains as popular and effective as ever.

The secret of its influence lies in the fact that its story of a fear-ridden girl setting off for the High Places in company with her much-loved Shepherd, is in fact the romance of Hannah's own personal pilgrimage.

This present account of her life begins with her Huguenot forebears, who left the lowlands of Europe for the flatlands of Essex more than 400 years ago, and recalls four generations of her remarkable family.

But its chief concern is to paint a vivid picture of this quite extraordinary Christian woman, who escaped from the prison house of her own morbid despair, and left for a new life of happy discipleship, first in the homeland, then in the Holy Land, where she served among both Jewish and Arab communities with incredible courage and skill.

At the heart of all her considerable achievements was a glowing and growing relationship with the One she had encountered so dramatically at the famous Convention at Keswick in the Lake District when she was just nineteen years of age.

But the story is not without its down side. Hannah had to wrestle with the loneliness of her single state, the tragic loss of her 55-year-old mother when she was twenty, and the raw wound of outraged jealousy when her father remarried. Then, once she had finished her work in Israel, and had begun to emerge as a writer destined to win fame on both sides of the Atlantic, all her relationships were thrown into turmoil by a radical shift in her theological outlook.

This book does not avoid the pains and perplexities of her later career, nor discount the new spheres of influence which opened up to her then. But it majors on those formative years of life when she exercised 'the ministry of reconciliation' during turbulent times in the Holy Land, and wrote those life-enhancing books which so many readers still gratefully treasure.

1 Ginger Beer and Poetry

Hannah made no bones about it. 'I was a miserable, morbid, self-centred person who never felt love for anyone', she later confessed. School was a torment. She could scarcely speak two words together without stammering. Her nights were haunted by numberless terrors. In the words of her friend, Mrs Bernadette Fletcher of Marco Island, Florida, 'Hannah lived in a cold, dark winterland of fear.'

Each Sunday as a small girl, she and her parents, plus their pet dog, would walk two miles to the Railway Mission in Colchester for morning worship. Then in the evening, they would attend a service in the Lexden Village Hall, which her grandmother had endowed.

She wanted for nothing. Her home was a handsome ten-bedroom house in an attractive village two miles west of Colchester. She was surrounded by a loving family. By any reckoning, they were rich.

But not even a 'decision' to follow Christ when she was eleven, could lighten the gloom of those sombre Sundays, or change the caste of her mind. Hannah was the original Miss Much-Afraid from the Fearing family of Much Trembling, so vividly described in her great book, *Hinds' Feet on High Places*.

No one could have guessed at that time, least of all Hannah herself, that one day this deeply unhappy young stammerer would enthral thousands of avid listeners, and would communicate the joy of discipleship to generations of grateful readers throughout a succession of best-selling books.

II

The Hurnards were of Huguenot stock. Their forebears had sailed to safety along the Colne into Colchester some time in 1571. A year later, on the eve of St Bartholomew's, August 23rd, 1572, thousands of their fellow Protestants in mainland Europe, were massacred.

Today, the Dutch quarter in Colchester, with its cluster of pastel-painted houses not far from the river, is quite select. But it is not difficult to imagine the settlement four centuries ago, when the crudely-plastered upper storeys of their dwellings hung over the mud tracks which then wound between the cottages.

Those Huguenots who settled in the town, brought strength of character, love of learning, and devotion to Scripture. Their industry led to the establishment of a thriving cloth trade in the area. One of their descendants, Charles Haddon Spurgeon (the surname is still familiar in Colchester) became the greatest Baptist preacher of the 19th century. Another, James Hurnard, who was Hannah's grandfather, became the town's most prodigious poet.

III

Like Hannah in later years, James Hurnard was an inveterate scribbler. His poems paint vivid word pictures of local life at a time when biographies of the town's worthies were few and far between; while his memoirs, ably edited by his widow, describe many fascinating characters in Hannah's own ancestry.

James's father, Robert, hailed from the village of Boreham, east of Chelmsford. He lived to the great age of ninety-one, and became what one journalist called 'a possessive, vain, compulsive chatterbox, even when deaf'! But in his early days, he had been a somewhat more bashful type.

Robert lost the love of his life just before they were due to be married. Some time later, he rode all of forty miles along narrow lanes through wide-rolling countryside, to the home of his uncle, Matthew Fennell, in Bury St Edmunds. He had no desire to form any romantic attachments. But Uncle wasted no time in arranging a meeting with a recent convert to the Quaker cause, Miss Hannah Clark.

Although she had many admirers, this daughter of a cele-brated beauty from Oxfordshire, also called Hannah, was 'a calm, unambitious' young lady 'with a discerning mind'. On October 7th, 1800, when Robert was twenty-six and Hannah thirty-two, they were married.

Their early life together was dogged by increasing finan-cial difficulty. The Napoleonic wars reduced the value of their land, and forced up the price of food. Hence, as their family increased, so did their debts. But their faith stood firm.

Nothing would keep Robert away from the Sunday morn-ing Meeting at Chelmsford, four miles from their home. One very wet weekend, his brother-in-law, Henry Clark, tried to persuade him to give it a miss. But Robert wouldn't hear of it. 'After all, I might pick up a fifty pound note on the way!' he joked. 'And did you?' Henry asked on his return. 'No,' he replied with some satisfaction, 'it was not a fifty pound note, but a hundred!' It seems that a Friend had informed him after the meeting, that a distant relative had left him a legacy for that amount.

But in the end, Robert and Hannah were forced to move. An attempt to make bricks out of his clay soil consumed too much of his dwindling capital. So, once they had settled in a little corner house by the village pump at Kelvedon in 1815, he walked to Little Baddow to look at a mill. On arrival, he discovered that his friend, Mark Whitehead, was there on precisely the same errand. They promptly went into partner-ship as millers.

But when their fortunes continued to decline, Robert and

Hannah set sail from Gravesend in April 1819 to seek a new life in America. For the eleven-year-old James, fourth of their children (Lucy, William Clark and Ann were the others) it was an adventure destined to end with his first close encounter with death. In the lovely little township of Wilmington, down by the Delaware river, his sister Lucy died of typhus. The melancholic young poet sought solace in the simplicity and certainty of his family's faith, and penned his tribute to her.

> But thy spirit is flown to the skies,
> To those mansions from misery free,
> Which are not for the brave, or the wise,
> But the pure and the humble like thee.

IV

Yet another legacy enabled the Hurnards to come back home in 1824. 'Thus after an absence of five years, all but a few days, did we find ourselves once more in old England', James wrote.

For a while they lived in Oxfordshire, from which his mother had hailed. And it was there that James came into a spiritual experience which was later to find its echo in his granddaughter's pilgrimage. 'I was walking one day in a lane near Henley, in a somewhat melancholy mood,' he wrote, 'when my heart was suddenly warmed with a divine influence. It seemed as if a holy glow pervaded my inmost soul. It was, I believe, a manifestation of the love of God to me. I felt His kindling presence, and, as I stood and leaned against a gate, tears of mingled joy and sorrow flowed from my eyes.'

However, he was delighted when the family decided to move back into their old corner house in Kelvedon. It meant that he could team up again with his great friends, Alfred and Louisa Bowman. His poem about 'friendship' uses the unfortunate expression 'happy hour' which has very different connotations nowadays when many a bar sells cut-price drinks at such a time! But his celebration of human companionship is timeless. It is also possible to recognise an old Essex accent in his rhyme for 'dawn'!

> The blackbird loves the close of day;
> The skylark loves the morning dawn;
> The nightingale the hour loves best
> When other birds to sleep are gone;
> The schoolboy loves the hour of play;
> The swain the hour his labours end;
> But oh! give me that happy hour,
> The happy hour when friend meets friend.

Sadly, the deaths of his sister Ann on February 7th, 1828, and his mother seven years later, plunged him once more into that dark depression which sometimes threatened to engulf him, and which his granddaughter Hannah may well have inherited.

There is no doubt at all that James disliked moving to Colchester, when later in 1828, his father hired a small brewery on East Hill, which is now a complex of well-appointed apartments. But for thirty-eight long years, James settled into the life mapped out for him, and dutifully 'strove to brew the best in all the thirsty town of Colchester'.

As the years passed by, James was required to care for an ageing and demanding father, when all the time he longed above all else to write a poetic masterpiece and gain recognition in his own right, then to find a loving wife.

V

But nothing can imprison the human mind. Those hours of contemplation spent at the Friends Meeting House in East Stockwell Street Sunday by Sunday, listening to the remorseless ticking of the clock, sensing the movement of the Holy Spirit, and applying his growing understanding of the Christian faith to the issues of the day, helped to shape his unswerving convictions.

At a time when Tories ruled unchallenged, James was a Liberal, and later, an Alderman. He labelled slavery 'the crowning crime of christendom'. In arguing, not merely for women to have the vote but to be able to stand for Parliament, he was far ahead of his time. The issue of free education for all, featured strongly in his writings. And although he brewed 'genuine, wholesome and invigorating ale', he hated drunkenness. Unusually for the times, he also disapproved of tobacco even though his father had been an inveterate pipe-smoker.

In the Garrison town of Colchester, James waged war on war itself. He was also scathing about lawyers who were 'sharp as well as cunning'. Those Bankers and Bishops who lived 'in princely luxury' were lashed by his pen.

But he warmed to Dr William Marsh, the godly Vicar of St Peter's on North Hill, through whose advocacy of work among Jewish people, Michael Solomon Alexander was first drawn towards the story of Jesus. Later, Alexander was to become the first Anglican Bishop in Jerusalem, and the first *Jewish* Bishop there in more than sixteen centuries.

At last, with the death of the old Patriarch Robert on January 7th, 1866, James felt free to make a life of his own. By the end of May that year, he had given up business. The brewery was now in the hands of Christopher Stopes, his Quaker friend who delighted in brewing ginger beer, and whose granddaughter was Marie Stopes, pioneer of birth control in Britain.

Before the year's end, James was back in his beloved Kelvedon. It was there, forty years after he had lost his heart to Louisa Bowman, who went on to marry Charles Smith of Coggeshall, that he proposed to her daughter, Louisa Bowman Smith. His cup of joy was full when on August 15th, 1867, the fifty-nine-year-old Quaker poet married his thirty-three-year-old sweetheart in the Friends Meeting House, Kelvedon.

2   *A Quaker Homestead*

Older residents in Lexden remember the grumbling tramcars which used to grind their way out of Colchester, and clank through their leafy village. The service started in 1904 the year before Hannah was born.

As the trams nosed out of the town along Crouch Street, they passed Endsleigh House on the corner of Wellesley Street. It was at Endsleigh that Hannah received her first schooling.

The route passed through imposing buildings on either side of the tree-lined Lexden Road, until, approaching the village itself, the trams gathered speed as they dipped downhill, past Hill House on the right, and the Parish Church on the left, before groaning uphill towards the terminus. It was at the junction with Straight Road, which runs to the left alongside some pre-Roman earthworks, that the trams used to reverse.

Nowadays, Hill House, at the heart of the old village, is a residential home for the elderly. But its history is far more exciting than its somewhat sedate exterior might suggest. At one time it had been owned by a crooked lawyer called Samuel Tillett, who had grown rich and become an Alderman of the Borough, by changing wills and conning farmers out of their savings. In 1850 he was rumbled and sent to Chelmsford jail.

Even that was not the end of his peccadilloes. He managed to get himself invalided out of prison, and presented at Court by the Duke of Wellington, no less. Unfortunately for Samuel, he happened to bump into the Judge who had sent him down and was promptly sent down again!

Inevitably, Tillett's house came up for sale, and having inherited a considerable fortune from a Quaker lady in 1872, James Hurnard, Hannah's grandfather, was able to acquire it.

Up until then, James and Louisa had lived over a shop at 6 Head Street, Colchester, having settled there after honey-mooning on the Isle of Wight in the summer of 1867. Revelling in his new-found happiness as a married man, James had been inspired to finish his epic poem on Victorian Colchester. The 10,200 lines, spread over 354 pages in seven books, finally saw the light of day during the early months of 1870. Today, his masterpiece, *The Setting Sun*, is a collector's item.

Then on August 17th that year, James and Louisa rejoiced in the birth of their one and only son, Samuel Fennell, Hannah's father. They moved into Hill House as a family on June 21st, 1873.

Shortly afterward, the previous owner of Hill House once more out of prison, was picked up by the police in London, having been found begging on the streets while dressed as a clergyman! The fact that his partner in crime was a prosti-tute, meant that Samuel Tillett, the former solicitor and his accomplice, were found guilty of unlawfully soliciting!

II

For the Hurnards, Hill House proved idyllic. The poet and his wife could look out of the bow windows to see the sturdy oaks of Lexden Park, the simple stone beauty of the village church, and the stirring sight of the Stage Coach thundering by.

Each day James would stroll down to the Lexden Springs behind the house, shaping thought into verse. Back in the gardens, Louisa and he loved to watch little Samuel play 'with ball, stick, or wheelbarrow'. Joy welled from within.

How full of love our hearts should be
   To Him our Heavenly Friend,
Who placed us in this happy home,
   Such peaceful days to spend.

There were frustrations too, of course. Poetry rarely sells well, and because the people of Colchester preferred 'fat beef and mutton' to literature, as he put it, he quite expected that his literary outpourings would be used 'to enwrap butter' rather than 'to enrapture the nation'! In this he wasn't to be disappointed!

More seriously, he and Louisa faced the prospect of losing the little lad who was the light of their eyes. At the age of six he fell ill with scarlet fever, and hovered on the brink of death. Mercifully he recovered. But as James himself was sixty-eight at the time, he realised all too well that late father-hood usually means early orphanhood.

Meanwhile, he rejoiced in all the simple pleasures of life in a place that he regarded as 'most picturesque of Essex villages'. He loved the smell of hay, the sight of green fields, the crackling of winter fire, and the taste of elder wine. As the railway now reached out to Colchester, he would listen for the hiss and roar of the train across the wide valley behind their home, and stand to watch 'the railway's fiery steed' speed toward London, just fifty-five miles away.

III

Four years before the Hurnards had moved into Hill House, an enterprising young Friend from the north had opened up a Quaker School in Lexden, with the help of John Kendall, a wealthy Quaker in Colchester.

As the school stood right next door to the grounds of Hill House, and was run by friends of his father, it was ideal for the young Samuel. So, once he was old enough, he was enrolled as a pupil. Part of the school premises still front on to the main road, though the taller building which once stood behind the present dwelling, has long since given way to modern development.

Samuel had unbounded respect for his sport-loving teacher, Frederick Richardson. Many years later, he joined forces with another former student, Edward N. Mennell to publish a twenty-eight page memoir of their school's founder and master. The original hand-written manuscript can still be seen in Colchester's Central Library.

By all accounts, Richardson was a born teacher, closely observing each pupil's personality, and adapting his approach accordingly. 'His mind was broad, his influence great', the tribute says.

Samuel enjoyed a sense of 'discovery' whatever subject Richardson taught. He particularly appreciated the simple experiments he set up in science lessons. He admired his teacher's skill as an archer, and says rather quaintly of his cricket, that he was 'an underarm twister'!

A fountain, erected by the boys, stands outside the church, commemorating Richardson's gifted son who died at the height of his powers.

Even after suffering a serious fall, Richardson used to ride to sporting events, enthusiastically calling out encouragement to his boys from the sidelines.

'The Governor', as the students called him, insisted that every boy should learn to swim. It is true that the river at Lexden was not ideal for swimming lessons. But it served its purpose. Samuel and Edward recall how some of the boys used to run the gauntlet of wasps on their way down to the river, when those who had run on ahead of them deliberately flicked their towels into the wasp nests along the way, thus annoying their inhabitants. Arms flailed in all directions as the stragglers battled to avoid being stung!

The little monograph paid tribute to Richardson's wife Sarah, who continued to wear the distinctive Quaker bonnet long after other ladies had stopped doing so. In the evenings, Sarah would read stirring stories to the young boarders at school. Older students recalled the impact made on them by the poems she sometimes recited at Sunday morning Meetings.

Samuel was just ten years old when his father James took ill in the night, and died at the age of seventy-two on February 26, 1881. One of the hymns James had written, focused on the Second Coming, a theme that was to dominate much of Samuel's ministry in future years:

> O Lord, Thy glorious day reveal,
>   The last and best of days!
> When all the sons of men shall kneel,
>   And shout one song of praise.

So the text chosen for his funeral could not have been more appropriate: 'Be ye also ready, for in such an hour as ye think not, the Son of Man cometh' (Matt 24:44, KJV). Significantly, it was not James's literary endeavours or political ambitions that received most comment that day (he had just become an Alderman). Instead, James Withers said of him:

> In works of charity his life was spent,
>   Did good by stealth, and 'blushed to find it fame';
> But these shall be his lasting monument,
>   And grateful memories will embalm his name.

Just over three years later, on April 20th, 1884, Samuel's mother died in her fifty-first year, and Samuel was thus left an orphan at the age of thirteen.

It could be significant that Samuel rarely wrote or spoke about his inner feelings. In later years, his wife would sometimes say to him, 'Why don't you just sit and talk with me this evening?' But he would reply, 'I have so much work that needs to be done today.' He channelled his very considerable energies into study, both at Ilkley College in Yorkshire, and Owens College, Manchester. After that, his life was filled with social and evangelistic work at home and overseas. Like

Hannah, his daughter, he also suffered from a speech imped-
iment, though it was never as severe as hers was to be.

IV

From a very early age, Samuel learned to assume responsibility. The Foundation Stone of Lexden Village Hall, now a
thriving Evangelical Church, records that the stone was laid
by Samuel Fennell Hurnard on September 25th, 1884. What it
does not say is that the stone-laying took place just five
months after his mother's death, and that Samuel himself
was in fact only fourteen years old at the time.

Those closest to him rarely remember him speaking about
his deepest feelings. His widow does not even know precisely
how and when he came into a living faith, though it is clear
that from a child he knew the Holy Scriptures which had
made him wise to salvation, and that his whole life was lived
as a devoted disciple of Jesus Christ.

It was his esteemed schoolmaster, Frederick Richardson,
who acted as Samuel's guardian during teenage years, equip-
ping him for college life in the north of England, and helping
to prepare him for the responsibilities of Christian leadership.

The legacy his father had inherited in 1872, plus the proceeds of his family's business ventures, ensured that he was
wealthy. But he always saw himself as a steward or trustee,
rather than as the 'owner' of such riches, and he lived as one
who would eventually be required to render account to God.
Scores of philanthropic and evangelistic agencies had cause
to thank God for the conscientiousness with which Samuel
discharged his trust.

He was a man of total integrity. One day in later years, his
wife came into the room to find the table littered with papers,
and Samuel engrossed in the accounts of a Society for which
he was Treasurer. 'Sh', he hissed when his wife's conversation threatened to disrupt his concentration. 'We are a half-
penny out.' It was typical of the man that he could not rest
until the missing money was found.

The Temperance Movement was gathering pace at this time, and Samuel continued his parents' involvement. James had warned against 'the serpent in the sparkling cup', and his wife Louisa had taken practical steps to offer an alternative. Not only did she endow the Village Hall, which was opened the year after her death, she also provided for a Temperance Hotel to be built next door to the Hall. It afforded comfortable accommodation and warm hospitality, but served only non-alcoholic drinks. The hotel is now a block of apartments.

There was a thriving Band of Hope at the Village Hall, where children took the pledge to avoid strong drink, and lustily sang the Band of Hope anthem:

> Dare to be a Daniel,
> Dare to stand alone,
> Dare to have a purpose firm,
> And dare to make it known.

Samuel himself was less political than his father James had been. It is hard to imagine him taking sides quite as publicly as his father had done, in what one critic has described as an 'opinionated manner' – as when, for example, he supported Bright and Gladstone, but deprecated that 'renegade' Disraeli who was so 'full of subtlety and cunning craft'!

But he was second to none in his devotion to civic duty. In 1895, at the age of twenty-five, Samuel was elected to the Lexden and Winstree Justices. Thereafter he served as JP on the bench of magistrates for fifty-two years, until, in 1947, he was removed to 'the supplemental list'.

As the local paper said of him, 'he was a man of strong character and driving force.'

V

It is hardly surprising that Samuel should suffer a breakdown in health during his twenties. The pressures on him were enormous. The doctor recommended him to take a cruise, and it was then that he met Rose Densham, the daughter of an aristocrat who owned a stately home on the Isle of Wight, and was on first name terms with members of the Royal Family.

Rose was a committed Christian, and when she proposed that services should be held on deck, the devout Samuel Hurnard inevitably became involved. Their shipboard romance blossomed, and they were married on her thirtieth birthday, March 3rd, 1899. After a honeymoon spent in Cornwall, they set up home together at Hill House.

Samuel was an evangelical Quaker. Eventually he was to part company from the local Meeting House because of what he perceived as its increasing liberalism, and was to find fellowship with the many interdenominational societies which clustered around the famous Keswick Convention.

Yet he never ceased to think of himself as a Quaker. His debt to the Society of Friends was incalculable. He co-edited the *Friends Witness* for a great many years. Even in everyday conversation he regularly used the characteristic 'thee' and 'thou' of Quaker-speak. Moreover he belonged to the Friends Prayer League founded in 1893, as also, later on, to the Friends Evangelistic Band.

There can be no doubt that Hill House, where Hannah Rose Hurnard first saw the light of day on May 31st, 1905, was very much a Quaker homestead.

3 *Little Miss Much-Afraid*

Sister Ruth was four, and Bracy nearly three, when Hannah came along. The arrival of Naomi just over three years later, made the family complete.

The children had everything going for them. Seven servants waited on their every need. Both parents were model Christians. Social and spiritual life at the Village Hall were flourishing. The private school Hannah attended, which later moved to Lexden Grange, before occupying The Park opposite Hill House, and eventually becoming the Sir Charles Lucas Comprehensive School, provided a quality education in which English, Scripture, Art and Music, featured strongly.

Yet all was not well for Hannah. It soon became obvious that she inherited something of her grandfather's melancholy, and a double dose of her father's stammer. As time went by, she came to live in a world of rebellious isolation.

Modern analysts might blame the strictness of her religious upbringing. Eventually, Hannah herself rejected some of those evangelical certainties which had proved so challenging to her as a small girl, but which had also driven her to seek the Kingdom of Heaven.

Her mother was an aristocratic lady who dressed well. People recall that, somewhat to the annoyance of her husband, she insisted on wearing a huge scarf for much of the time. Maybe Samuel thought she was always dressed for leaving home, whereas she was simply afraid of catching cold! Her health was never robust.

In between bouts of pain and nervous prostration, Rose would take the platform and command attention. She had a penchant for thinking theologically and a flair for words. As a public speaker, she was much in demand.

But as far as Hannah was concerned, her greatest sermons were preached in the home. 'As for my mother,' she wrote in *The Hearing Heart*, 'through all the years of her ill-health, suffering and almost constant pain, she was so joyful a "lover" of the Lord Jesus that when she spoke His name her very voice changed and her face became lighted as though an inner lamp shone through the inner vessel. "His Name is as ointment poured forth, therefore do we love him", is the verse which I most closely associate with her memory.'

Yet for all the devoted and patient care of both parents, Hannah's heart was in rebellion. Metaphorically speaking, she suffered from crippled feet and a crooked mouth. Her petrifying speech defect cut her off even from those who wanted to shower their love on her; while her attempts to walk in the Christian way proved disastrous. She had been told often enough that the Bible was dynamite. But she found it dull. The promised salvation never seemed to materialise.

The grey brick house in which Hannah lived, stood opposite a cold stone church; and on a wintry day under a spitting sky, the scene perfectly mirrored the greyness of her inner self. The sight of wind-blown leaves scudding along the street, symbolised for her a life at the mercy of 'fate'.

When the time came to go to bed each evening, Hannah feared the inevitable nightmares that would follow, and dreaded she might wake up in outer darkness. Just occasionally there were intimations of better things. She loved animals, especially her pet rabbit 'Peter'. And an occasional visit to Mersea Island, just ten miles away, would briefly lighten her spirit. At such times, she stopped feeling unhappy. But on most days, the growing girl could only squirm with embarrassment at not being able to answer a question at school, or talk to a grown-up who was trying to make her feel wanted.

Sometimes she wished she had enough courage to commit suicide. 'Till I was nineteen,' she wrote, 'I never remember feeling happy.'

II

Hannah's social status undoubtedly cut her off from most of her peers. Her mother came from the aristocracy: her father was 'a gentleman of independent means', and in the early part of the twentieth century, such people did not mingle too readily with the *'hoi polloi'*! It was not always a case of snobbery on one side, or subservience on the other: more a feeling that each person must fulfil the role assigned to him or her in life, and that society would fall apart unless everybody kept his place and did his duty.

So Hannah felt at a distance from most young people of her own age. Even the boys from the Quaker school next door, who wound their way up hill to a Gospel service in the Village Hall each Sunday evening, or came to functions held on the lawns of Hill House, would not have felt totally at ease in the company of exalted people like the Hurnards!

So it is unlikely that Hannah took a great deal of notice when Marjorie Eady came on the scene in 1917, for example, even when she attended the children's meeting at six o'clock every Friday evening in the Village Hall.

Marjorie and her twin, Florence, had been born at West Bergholt, some seven miles away, but moved into Spring Lane at the bottom of the hollow near Hill House, when Marjorie was seven and Hannah nearly fourteen.

'My father was "Chapel",' Marjorie says. 'Originally he came from Lavenham, a Huguenot wool town over the border in Suffolk. But my mother was Church of England, and I went with her. I used to help her clean the brasses at St Leonard's. But the children's meeting up at the Hall on Friday evenings, took my interest. I was converted there when I was ten through Mr Hopkins, the Army Scripture Reader. He spoke about the Second Coming. I knew I wasn't ready. So I asked the Lord to save me. I can remember Mr Hopkins now, dressed in his uniform. He looked very smart.'

Marjorie treasures the certificate which records her Confirmation at St Peter's on North Hill in Colchester. 'The Vicar would ask each Confirmation candidate in turn what it means to be a Christian. He knew from the replies he got which ones had really come to know the Lord as Saviour,' Marjorie observes. 'But eventually I joined the Village Hall, and started teaching in the Sunday School there. I remember Mrs Hurnard well, and Hannah too, of course.'

But quite apart from the six-and-a-half year difference in their ages, Marjorie and Hannah moved in different worlds. There was a social divide which would have prevented them becoming close friends at that time.

Other people thought it a great honour to be a Hurnard! But it put pressure on the younger members of the family. They certainly had a lot to live up to. Much was expected of them. Moreover, their status in life set them apart from others.

III

The outbreak of war over the August Bank Holiday in 1914, could only add to the nine year old Hannah's seemingly endless store of crippling fears. Pacifists were regarded as little less than traitors. So many Quakers faced ostracism, or worse.

Meanwhile, lads from Lexden left for the war. Within a matter of months, casualties mounted. The first bomb dropped on London at the beginning of October. One month later, 700 men died when their ship, HMS *Bulwark*, was blown up in Sheerness Harbour, some forty miles from Colchester. Nearer still, a village policeman in Essex arrested the German crew of a crashed Zeppelin one morning, before going on traffic duty in the afternoon! But the war was getting uncomfortably close to the ever-fearful Hannah.

Charlie Chaplin's film *The Tramp* went on release in 1915, but Hannah would not have been allowed to see it. The Hippodrome in Colchester, like all other places of public entertainment, was out of bounds. The Hurnards believed in total separation from the world.

Yet 'separation' was not interpreted as 'withdrawal'. They believed that Christians were meant to be *in* the world, even though they were no longer *of* it. Hence, Hill House became a centre for social caring and gospel preaching during the war.

One old faded sepia photograph, dated 1917, shows a crowd of soldiers on the lawn. Several prim servants, demurely dressed in starched white aprons, stand towards the back. Left of centre is the patriarchal figure of Samuel Hurnard, his pet cockatoo perched on his left shoulder. Just in front of him is the twelve year old round-faced Hannah. Right in the foreground is Mr Prentice, with the baby organ he had played when teaching the men a popular chorus of the time:

> Just the same, just the same,
> The God who lived in Moses' time
> Is just the same today.

Sure enough, the men soon made up some lines of their own once they had mastered the tune. Their rendering owed more to the ubiquitous corned beef of army rations than it did to the teaching they'd heard on the lawns of Hill House!

> Just the same, just the same,
> The bully beef of Moses' time
> Is just the same today!

It so happens that the fruit trees in the beautiful gardens of Hill House yielded in abundance that year. So the Hurnards were able to serve up lavish helpings of cherry plum pie to the hungry soldiers. It more than made up for the boring diet in the mess.

The three Hurnard daughters also added some entertain-

ment of their own, as Hannah recalled in one of her little
booklets written during the seventies:

> When I was a little girl during the First World War, we all lived
> in the Garrison town of Colchester, and every weekend dur-
> ing the summer months my parents used to ask large groups
> of soldiers to high tea in the garden, followed by a service for
> them in a big tent which was erected on the lawn. How inter-
> ested we children always were when we watched the tent
> being erected, the curtains looped skilfully over the poles,
> with the canvas roof attached, and slowly hauled up to the
> erect position and held firmly in place by tightly drawn cords
> attached to pegs driven strongly into the earth, and the flap-
> ping canvas sides then skilfully secured like skin around the
> bones, and the tabernacle was secure and ready for the sum-
> mer. They were happy times for us children. The soldiers all
> delighted in being in a home again, and playing with us and
> with my father's white and gold crested Australian cockatoo
> which walked about among us and on the seats, quite as
> much at home as anyone else; and the pet white rats with
> pink eyes which we little girls would put up our dress sleeves
> while an admiring throng of soldiers gathered round and
> waited with cheers of encouragement to greet them when the
> little creatures finally ran down the other arm and emerged
> into view again!

Better still, the Tabernacle on the lawn became the place
where many of the men found their way to faith in Christ as
a result of the meetings held in it.

IV

As the war drew to a close, weary survivors returned home
with stories to tell of savagery on the Somme, or triumphs in
the East. One old soldier in Colchester, well-known to the
Hurnards, used to tell of General Allenby's exploits in
Palestine. At 4.30 on the morning of September 19th, 1918,
the young soldier had served himself breakfast on the Plain
of Sharon by lopping oranges off the trees with his sword,
before riding north with Allenby's Cavalry Brigade to help

capture Megiddo by 7.30 am, and Nazareth by 2.30 in the afternoon.

That Palestine campaign, described by Encyclopaedia Britannica as being one of the greatest cavalry battles in history, was to have a marked effect on evangelical thinking at that time. For many devout students of biblical prophecy, it heralded a significant step forward in God's unfolding purposes. Such happenings certainly quickened and deepened Samuel's teaching on the Second Coming. In Hebrew, Armageddon is *Har Megiddo*: 'Mountain of Megiddo' (Rev 16:16, Living Bible).

Meanwhile, in society at large, war was to change all kinds of social attitudes. Inevitably the bonds of morality were loosened. And now that men and women had served together in the armed forces, or worked side by side in factories, old social conventions were almost bound to change. And they did.

In 1918, Dr Marie Stopes, whose grandfather had lodged with James Hurnard, Hannah's grandfather, and was in fact his business partner, wrote a book called *Married Love*, in which she called for more openness about sexuality, and demanded that contraception be more widely available.

Such ideas would have been anathema to Hannah's puritan parents, and went far beyond Hannah's own personal priorities. But she had the normal instincts of a young adolescent, and was surrounded by any number of young fellows at the Village Hall. In *Hinds' Feet on High Places*, Miss Much-Afraid speaks to the Shepherd about her 'great longing to experience the joy of natural, human love, and to learn to love supremely one person who will love me in return.'

But it was not to be. Later on there was a romance, though where, when and with whom, remain a mystery. But Hannah came to realise that her dreams were destined to be set aside, and that her whole being was to belong exclusively to Another. As she wrote in *Hinds' Feet*, 'the seed of love which her Shepherd gave to her was a thorn which matched the scars in His hand.'

V

But whatever psychological, social and sexual factors might have contributed to the wretchedness Hannah suffered, there can be no doubt that the underlying cause was spiritual.

On the one hand, she recognised the validity of her parents' faith, and admired the quality of their respective characters. On the other hand, she resented the restraints and restrictions which their puritan lifestyle imposed.

There was no shortage of Christian input so far as the children were concerned. There were family prayers at home. Both the Village Hall at Lexden, and the Railway Mission on North Hill in Colchester, throbbed with spiritual life. The Gospel was preached most emphatically. There were regular conversions. Bible teaching was strongly emphasised. Samuel himself wrote a little commentary on 'The Revelation' in 1920, when Hannah was just fifteen, and this was later expanded and republished. The cause of 'Temperance' was taken up with vigour. Famous missionaries and ministers preached in the Village Hall and stayed at Hill House. Practical help in the form of groceries and coal, was given to the poorer members of the community. Garden parties were held on the lawns of Hill House.

Above all, Christians were summoned to a life of total commitment. As Hannah wrote in the opening sentence of *The Hearing Heart*, 'I was brought up in an Evangelical home and environment where religious beliefs were considered far and away the most important things in the world.'

Every week, Samuel would travel to London two or three times for committees, conferences or annual meetings. Eventually he became Treasurer of at least fifteen missionary societies, as well as being Chairman of the Mazawattee Tea Company. He was also a local magistrate. Any number of worthy causes made claims on his time. It was also necessary for him to study, prepare, and edit the *Friends Witness*. At the same time, his wife ran the household, and exercised a wide-ranging ministry of her own. The children must have felt overwhelmed by such a plethora of activity. How could they possibly live up to such high standards of complete dedication?

It was, of course, the very *intensity* of this commitment which provoked such a strong resistance in each of the children. 'We all experienced as we grew to adolescence and adulthood,' she wrote, 'a most violent reaction and antagonism to this environment and outlook.'

In her own case, rebellion resulted in agnosticism. She had given herself to 'the unseen Saviour' when she was about eleven, without at the same time facing up to 'the unseen sin' of resentment against both her physical limitations and psychological hang-ups. There had been 'decision' without repentance. Hence she failed to find the peace she sought, and felt 'let down' by God.

Yet her father in particular always treated her with special tenderness. He knew from his own experience the humiliations caused by a stammering tongue. But he longed for his daughter to experience an inner release. So he planned to take her to the great Christian Convention which is held at Keswick in Cumbria every July. He knew that she would bridle at the whole idea of attending yet more 'meetings' *ad infinitum*. But he struck a bargain with her. 'Hannah, my dear, if we stay for a further week in the beauties of the Lake District, wilt thou accompany me to the Keswick Convention this year?' he enquired.

He took some comfort from Hannah's rather resigned and reluctant 'yes'. Neither he nor she were to realise the full implications of that particular decision.

4   Damaged Reed and Smouldering Wick

I

To anyone brought up in the gentle countryside of north Essex, with its wide vistas and big skies, but no great heights, the Lake District is another world. There are mountains at the end of almost every street in Keswick. Derwentwater sparkles in the sunlight. Boats nose their way through the waters to rocky knolls, tree-crowned islands, and shaded bays.

There is a lifting of the heart in the sweep of the fells. Sheep wander at will. Walkers trek up Skiddaw. Clouds paint patterns on the hillsides. And God is everywhere.

Each July, the town of Keswick is taken over by hordes of Bible-loving Christians. The tent in Skiddaw Street, now modernised, fills up with eager worshippers. Friends greet each other warmly. It is a familiar rendezvous. Some people come here unfailingly every year. For them there is nowhere better to find splendid teaching, inspired singing, rich fellowship, and missionary fervour.

It isn't everyone's cup of tea, of course. The Convention has been assailed by clever critics, crusty theologians, or hyped-up radicals ever since it first began. But it has shown an amazing ability to beguile many of its most trenchant opponents, several of whom have gone on to become some of its most persuasive advocates.

Hannah arrived on Saturday July 19th, 1924 for the start of what was the 49th Convention. Her father was completely at home, of course. He was involved in any number of those evangelical agencies which found their focus of fellowship in the Keswick movement.

Moreover, the Quaker influence had been present from the very outset of the Convention, since the co-founder had been Robert Wilson, a burly bearded Friend from Cockermouth. He had been the person responsible for choosing Keswick's on-going slogan: *All One in Christ Jesus* (Gal 3:28). And his own lifestyle had been a living commentary on those words. Each Sunday morning he would worship with the Quakers. In the afternoon he taught in the local Baptist Sunday School. Then in the evening he would attend the Parish Church.

Keswick was ecumenical long before it was popular to be so, and unlike some other special 'Weeks', has resisted the ever-present peril of hiving off from the mainstream churches to become a quasi denomination in its own right.

Part of the pleasure in attending the Convention is to meet notable figures from so many different denominations, as they stroll along the streets, chatting with interested well-wishers, and passing the time of day with all and sundry.

Bishop Taylor Smith was a familiar sight, bustling along the road dressed in episcopal gear and wearing his silver-rimmed pince-nez. He had been Queen Victoria's favourite preacher, and he was always in demand as a counsellor, especially by young people. The official report of that 1924 Convention says that while he would set out early for a meeting, he would sometimes not arrive until it was almost over. Mercifully, that didn't appear to happen on those occasions when he was due to speak!

Once on the platform, the portly Bishop sat among fellow-speakers like Montague Goodman from the Christian Brethren; F.B. Meyer, John MacBeath, and W.Y. Fullerton from the Baptists; and Charles Inwood, a Methodist Minister who had served in Ireland.

As usual, the panel of speakers that year was international as well as interdenominational. W.Y. Fullerton hailed from Ireland, and was destined to become Home Secretary of the

Baptist Missionary Society. W.H. Aldis, speaking at Keswick for the first time, was involved in the China Inland Mission, now the Overseas Missionary Fellowship. Yet another first-timer, Bishop Linton, served in Persia (Iran).

Indeed, the missionary element could not possibly be avoided, since among the huge crowds that thronged the streets and filled the tents, there were literally hundreds of Christian workers from all over the world. A great many of them had first heard their call to serve overseas through the ministry of the Convention.

II

But while Samuel was in his element, Hannah shrivelled up inside. She loved the mountains, of course. As a girl, she had enjoyed three family holidays in Switzerland before the First World War. And just a few months before coming to Keswick, she had spent a term at a school in Horgen, near Zurich. But she hated crowds at the best of times, and while there were plenty of quiet places down by the lake or up on the hills for those seeking solitude, the meetings themselves were chock-a-block.

She looked into the faces all around her, and was infuriated by their ever-ready smiles! If only she could escape from this suffocating atmosphere to find freedom in the beauties of lakeland! But she had made an agreement with her father to attend one meeting each morning, and another each evening. So the ordeal could not be avoided. In any case, it rained a lot that week, so the hills were invisible for much of the time.

Mercifully, the atmosphere of the Convention that year was remarkably relaxed. Two years previously, Douglas Brown had come fresh from the 1921 East Anglian Revival, and his Bible Readings were said to have been more like bombshells! At least Hannah did not have to cope with lots of undue excitement. In fact the Keswick Report for 1924 commented that it was 'a quiet and apparently, on the surface, an uneventful week': admirably suited, one would think, for a nineteen year old Quaker girl in distress of soul.

Moreover, the dominant theme of the week seems to have been that of 'encouragement'. In an address that was rather typical, Bishop Linton reminded his hearers that Messiah does not shout or cry out, or raise his voice in the streets. 'A bruised reed shall he not break, and the smoking flax shall he not quench' (Isa 42:3, KJV). The picture is of a shepherd mending the damaged reed in his pipe, instead of throwing it away, and of a peasant woman filling up her empty clay oil lamp, so that the smouldering wick should burst into flame once more. So too, the Lord restores the lost chord of joy in the Christian's heart, and makes his witness bright again.

The Bible readings by W.Y. Fullerton which were one of the two series given at noon each day, ungirded this emphasis on 'the God of all comfort'. J.C. Pollock describes how Fullerton 'took a little innocent pride in preaching without notes, Bible in hand, perfectly at ease before the great audience'. But after all these years, his Readings still have the power to speak to the heart.

The studies were based on Isaiah 53 – 55, where the Suffering Servant atones for His people's sins (53), comforts them in all their fears (54), and provides the perfect antidote to their doubts (55).

Significantly, Fullerton finished his studies with a quotation from George Fox, founder of the Quaker movement, which summed up all that the Keswick Convention stood for, and which could not have been bettered as a prescription for Hannah's troubled heart, even though she was not yet ready to open up to it:

> I knew Jesus and He was very dear to me, but I found something in my heart that would not be sweet and kind and patient. One day I asked Him if He could do anything for me, and He came into my heart, and He took out of it all that would not be kind and sweet and patient, and then – He shut the door.

III

The week dragged by interminably for Hannah. Only glimpses of glory in nature relieved the torment of those teeming crowds and evangelical exhortations.

But the three hour Missionary Meeting on Saturday morning, July 26th, was altogether different. The young would-be agnostic could not resist the wisdom and the Spirit by which the missionaries spoke.

W.Y. Fullerton presided. The strains of 'The Old Hundredth' filled the tent. Isaiah 49 was read. John MacBeath led in prayer.

The gospel is *'first for the Jew'* (Rom 1:16). So it was Dr Orr-Ewing from the Christian Hospital in Jerusalem, who gave the opening talk. He mentioned the difficulties faced when fourteen different languages are being used in the one hospital! But then he spoke of the greater problems faced by Jewish people who come to faith in Jesus as Messiah. 'Would *you* be baptised if your wife was thus automatically divorced from you? If you lost your children? If you lost your work? If you were socially ostracised?' he asked.

There were reports from India, China and Japan. Then, after prayer, envelopes were distributed throughout the tent. More speakers followed describing work in Paraguay, among Indians in Canada, and in Uganda.

At twelve o'clock the meeting paused to offer up prayer for the whole world. Then Dr Fraser spoke about pioneer work in southern Sudan – one of today's martyr Churches. As the great crowd sang with missionary fervour 'I hear ten thousand voices singing', the envelopes, now filled with gifts and promises, were collected up.

Still the interest did not flag. Miss Florence Miller, a pioneer missionary living and working among Muslims in northern Nigeria, without the support of any missionary society, spoke of the threats and opportunities she faced. Miss Lilian Trotter prayed. Then Bishop Linton of Persia (Iran) talked about Christian life in a land that was ninety-five per cent

Muslim, and called for volunteers to serve in any number of different capacities and to pray 'God guide me'.

The meeting drew to a close. First W.Y. Fullerton asked all serving missionaries to stand. Hundreds did so. Then he asked all those training to serve overseas, to stand as well. The crunch came when he echoed the Bishop's appeal: 'If God opens up the way, are you willing to go at His bidding?' Almost at once, some 250 young people stood up in all parts of the great tent. When parents were asked to stand if they were willing to let their children serve 'in foreign fields' should God call them, Hannah became conscious that her dearly loved father was rising to his feet.

'That was the last straw,' Hannah wrote. 'I struggled to my feet and hurried out of the tent. Getting on my bicycle I tore back to our lodging-house outside the town, rushed into my little room, and locking the door fell on my knees beside the bed.' She wrestled in prayer. The birth pangs of a new life had begun in earnest.

Meanwhile, the congregation in the tent sang a final hymn

> Set on fire our heart's devotion,
> With the love of Thy dear name,
> Till o'er every land and ocean
> Lips and lives Thy cross proclaim.

5 *Warfare Ended: Sin Forgiven*

The idea that Hannah would ever make a missionary was quite preposterous, of course. Whatever was her father thinking of? She could scarcely put a sentence together without stuttering unmercifully, while her faith was virtually non-existent.

But in one half hour on Saturday July 26th, 1924, the nine-teen year old's world was turned on its head. No one could match Hannah's own account in *The Hearing Heart* of what happened in her digs that lunch time. Suffice it to say that she heard the Shepherd's call to leave for the High Places.

There on her knees, she did what no counsellor would ever recommend: she opened her Bible at random to seek a word from the Lord. But when a person is drowning, almost any kind of life-line will do, and in *her* case, it worked! The Bible fell open at 1 Kings 18, and challenged her to stop limp-ing between faith and unbelief (v 21). Now was the time for her to make up her mind once and for all.

The passage also called for action. 'If the Lord is God, *fol-low* Him' (KJV), she read, with an emphasis on the verb. Heaven alone knew where it all would end. But in the final analysis, you only find out whether any given road is the right one, by taking it: a person can only discover whether the teaching of Jesus is truly from heaven, by actually obeying it (John 7:17).

At the same time, Hannah was all too conscious that the

story of Elijah speaks of an altar. She had to face the fact that a cost was involved. In particular, the Shepherd might be asking her to become a 'communicator', stammer and all. 'I can only say that THAT WAS THE THOUGHT THAT CAME TO ME WITH TERRIBLE TORTURING CLARITY', she wrote in *The Hearing Heart* (p 17).

It would have helped if she could have felt some sense of God's nearness. But she was having to face the issue on her own, with no more props. It was then that she read verse 38 with new eyes, for only as Elijah stood alone and doused the altar with water, did the fire of the Lord fall. And the message struck home.

By now she was crying copiously, so that just as the prophet's altar on Mount Carmel was saturated with water, so her hour of self-offering was bathed with tears. At the same time, the love of Jesus began to burn in her. 'Into my lonely, dark, tormented heart, there flooded, like a burst of sunshine, the realisation that has never left me,' she wrote. 'Jesus is real. He is here. He loves me, even me' (p 18).

The Shepherd had come to her in the Valley of Humiliation. 'Now you will be able to go with me to the High Places and be a citizen in the Kingdom of my Father', He had said (*Hinds' Feet*, p 17).

II

The Young Peoples' Meetings held every evening at Keswick during Convention week were always popular. To start with, they were short. There were no long drawn out sermons, but tuneful choruses followed by brief talks which dealt with issues of concern to the many hundreds of young people camped out all week under canvas in nearby fields, or staying in one of the numerous guest houses around town.

The meetings were also late in the day (9.00 p.m.) and reserved exclusively for the under thirties. Young people could mingle with folks of their own age, with no venerable worthies hovering around with well-meaning words of advice drawn from their long experience!

Above all, the talks were very practical. Clarence Foster, for example, knew the kind of things which bugged young people, and could use basic problems to highlight deeper realities.

For the first time that she could ever remember, Hannah was actually eager to get to a Christian meeting! She had taken her first tentative steps towards the High Places. Now she needed all the help she could get. And that evening, Clarence Foster's talk gave her the vital blueprint for her future lifestyle.

In those days, Keswick emphasised the need for a daily 'Quiet Time', and in so doing, introduced whole generations of young people to the daily discipline of reading the Bible and praying every morning. Clarence Foster spoke about the ingenious methods some young folks used to help them get out of bed early so they could have their 'Quiet Time'. But then he put a whole new slant on the practice by likening 'the Morning Watch' to a meeting between lovers.

Hannah had decided that it was unlikely she would ever have a boyfriend. 'Morbid, abnormal people, and people who stammer, possibly, may not have human lovers,' she later wrote in *The Hearing Heart* (p 24). But what if prayer is meeting with your dearest friend, and reading the Bible is like devouring His love-letter to you? Then it obviously affects the whole question of daily prayer, for who would want to lie in bed and so miss a personal encounter with the One whose love alone makes life worth living?

III

Samuel's joy matched her own when she shared her experience with him and said that she wanted to go to Bible College. But the Fearing family who had invaded her mind over the years, were rather less than pleased. Her spiritual experience did not suddenly change her human disposition. 'Craven Fear' still threatened to take her over!

> With a horror that sickened her very heart she heard him say, 'Well, here you are at last, little Cousin Much-Afraid. So we are to be married, eh, what do you think of that?' and he pinched her, presumably in a playful manner, but viciously enough to make her gasp and bite her lips to keep back a cry of pain (*Hinds' Feet*, p 20).

For two and a half months, Hannah pondered the prospect of leaving home and going to Bible College in south west London. Then for the first time in her life, she travelled to the capital on her own, negotiating the underground (metro) system, and hailing a taxi. Asking for 'Ridgelands Bible College' in Wimbledon was an ordeal in itself because the letters 'r' and 'w' were specially difficult for her to enunciate. But she had already discovered that whenever there was a challenge to face, the necessary strength was available to her. As she had learned during a Beach Mission near home where she had assisted during the summer once Keswick was over: I CAN'T...GOD CAN. Indeed 'I can do all things through Christ who strengthens me' (Phil 4:13).

There were many times in that first term when she had to put this principle into practice. She revelled in the chance to mix with so many keen young Christians, and to study the Scriptures at greater depth. A number of the lecturers were Keswick speakers, men like E.L. Langston, the College Chairman, W.W. Martin, and Graham Scroggie. So the teaching fed her spirit, as well as stimulating her mind. And provided she did not get involved in any long or deep conversations, she could make do with 'yes' and 'no', or some other relatively easy monosyllable. At least she did not have to answer questions in class, as she had tried to do at Endsleigh School! But such wiles and stratagems could not answer every eventuality, or disguise for ever the real situation.

The crunch came when her name was posted up as one of

the four trialists at the 'Speakers Class' held by the Principal, Mrs Howard Hooker, on the second or third Thursday of her very first term.

Immediately the Fearing family of Much-Trembling began to bully her! At first she threw a panic when she saw her name on the list. But then she applied the new rule of her discipleship, and set to work preparing a three-headed address on what had become her favourite text: 'My grace is sufficient for thee: for my strength is made perfect in weakness' (2 Cor 12:9, KJV).

Though she did not realise it at the time, it was really in her favour that the ordeal would not be hanging over her for ever and a day! The experience of giving a message and having it mulled over by staff and students alike, would soon be over for good.

When the day arrived, the miracle happened. She stood in front of the class, announced her text, and gave her talk with scarcely a hesitation, let alone a stammer. The students, expecting to suffer the acute embarrassment of hearing a stuttering novice, could only look on her with astonishment and delight. Her 'sermon' was such a success that Mrs Hooker remarked on her gift for public speaking!

From that point onward, Miss Much-Afraid was quite unrecognisable as the blushing stammerer who had run away from crowds. She would preach in the open air, teach in Sunday School, or address any number of women's meetings with something approaching confidence.

The stutter sometimes surfaced again when she was tired or under stress. She could never take the new freedom to speak for granted. If she ceased to lean hard on the Lord, as she put it, she could find herself mugged by one or other of the Fearing family, and left in tatters. But whenever she cried out to the Shepherd as a matter of urgency, His stern face and strong cudgel would make even Craven Fear lose his grip and cringe away (*Hinds' Feet*, p 21). In fact, one of her fellow students once said to her 'I almost envy you your stammer Hannah, it seems to keep you so close to Him, and make Him so real to you, whereas I am always slipping away into unreality, and trying to manage without Him' (*The Hearing Heart*, p 32).

IV

Once her two year course at Ridgelands was over, Hannah joined the Friends Evangelistic Band (FEB), an evangelistic agency still at work in Britain, but known now as FEBV (The Fellowship for Evangelising Britain's Villages).

The Society had started less than seven years before Hannah joined, when a chemist's assistant from Cornwall, who had been Secretary of The Friends Prayer League since 1909, and shared the same name as the first Quaker, George Fox, led a team of five people on an evangelistic venture in Darlington way up in the north of England.

Ever since it began in 1893, the Friends Prayer League, of which Samuel Hurnard was a prominent member, had expressed concern that so much evangelism was seemingly ineffective. One of the founders had said to his colleague while they travelled by train one day: 'Friend, the begetting power of the Spirit is strangely absent from much of the preaching of the gospel in our day.' The immediate effects of the 1859 revival had waned. Now it seemed that while children came to birth, there was 'no strength to deliver them' (Isa 37:3).

So, for twenty-six years, the Prayer League had given itself to the ministry of intercession. Then, as they became convinced that 'a prayer league without a missionary movement is incomplete,' the FEB came into being.

That Darlington mission led by Fox, won the support of many Ministers in the town, and as it was bathed in prayer, it was blessed with power. Within a year, similar efforts were held in a dozen different places near and far including the Channel Islands. But as time went by, many unfamiliar place names began to appear in the published reports! The Friends Evangelistic Band had discovered its main ministry: reaching out with the good news into the numberless villages where 'closed chapels abounded, dirty and overgrown, where sin went unrebuked, the sick and aged were not visited, children had no Sunday Schools and adults no services' (Bryers, p 35).

It was not always easy for members of the Band to find accommodation when they visited an area. But in 1923, three years before Hannah joined the work-force, a motor caravan had been donated to the work and dedicated to the Lord at Bury St Edmunds. By the time Hannah joined the team of twenty workers in 1926, two horse-drawn caravans (trailers) had been added to the fleet! Four years later, there were forty vans and nearly a hundred workers.

So it was that the twenty-one year old fledgling evangelist exchanged the luxury of Hill House, and the excitement of a London College, for the adventure of life in a lonely village, living in a 'home on wheels'.

6 *In the Service of the Shepherd*

Hannah always looked back to those four years spent in FEB as 'radiant with a golden light, like an early summer morning, sparkling with dew, and full of singing birds' (*The Hearing Heart*, p 35).

Some members of her family were shocked by Hannah's new gypsy lifestyle, which was hardly surprising! Her colleague for some of the time, Suzette Poole, says that it must have been startling for Hannah herself 'to be wakened in the morning by a large pig rubbing against the caravan wheel' in a farmer's field at Tolleshunt D'Arcy in Essex!

But Hannah could not have been happier. The old gloom had gone for good. New adventures awaited her every day. And she was in the will of God.

There were battles too, of course. The *Friends Witness*, co-edited by her father, carried reports of FEB work each month, quoting extracts from field reports and telling of opposition in many quarters. There could be indifference too. In late 1926, Hannah and a new colleague, Phyllis Jones, found that the folks at Bircher Common in Shropshire preferred dances and whist drives in the Community Hall, to mission services in the village chapel! But they battled through, and people started coming. 'Last night, in spite of the devil doing his worst, we had a very grand and solemn time; people were visibly awed,' Hannah wrote in January 1927.

It is astonishing how many miles they covered. In spite of

wintry conditions, January 1927 found the new worker busy in Lincolnshire on the east, as well as Shropshire (twice) in the west. During March, they joined several other colleagues for a much bigger mission at Leominster, not far from the Welsh border. Then in June, Hannah and Suzette crossed the Irish Sea to work in Bray and Dublin.

But Suzette at least appreciated those occasions when their caravan was parked in an Essex village within reach of Colchester. It gave them the chance to cycle over to Hill House in Lexden on a free Saturday, 'to stretch their arms', as Samuel put it, and to luxuriate in a hot bath!

They sometimes stayed in a given area of the country for several weeks, breaking down barriers, and building up contacts. Most clergy cooperated happily when Hannah and her colleague called at the local Manse or Vicarage to introduce themselves. But there were exceptions. The Minister of a nonconformist chapel in rural Oxfordshire, in the heart of England, refused the use of his church hall for a mission during the summer of 1929. So Hannah and Winifred Harvey, her colleague at the time, decided to concentrate on door-to-door visitation, with the result that every home in the village was visited, literature was distributed to all and sundry, children's meetings were held on street corners and people were brought to faith through meetings held on the green, or by one-to-one talks in the home.

Each August, students from Ridgelands Bible College, where Hannah had studied, gained experience by working alongside FEB members during the long summer vacations.

II

Life in FEB was a learning experience for Hannah too. Indeed she garnered more practical wisdom from life in the Band than she could ever have gained from any college or book.

Village life has its own close network of relationships, and strangers have to tread warily. Hannah learned to relate to people, win their confidence, allay their fears and speak to their needs.

Then too, it took considerable courage for a reticent person, who continued to wrestle with a 'thorn in the flesh', to visit local dignitaries in a new area, and to become accepted within the community at large.

Sometimes the courage required was of a very physical kind. In the 'wild west' of County Sligo in Ireland, where Protestants were anathema, Hannah and Suzette took over a caravan which had bullet holes in it. The FEB men who'd used it last had been fired on. Moreover no Catholic worth his salt would have been seen dead in the cleaned-up white-washed chicken shed which the intrepid couple used as their mission hall! But they held their meetings just the same, in spite of the stones raining down on the corrugated iron roof. At length they won the respect of the villagers, who then plied them with so many gifts of fruit, vegetables and provisions, that they had to use their hand cases in order to carry them home!

FEB workers needed to be adaptable. So Hannah found herself pedalling and playing the portable fold-down pneumatic harmonium! She also learned how to address different kinds of audiences. Visiting the sick and dying, witnessing to the weak or the wicked, all required special skills honed by experience.

But the work was never drudgery. There was a song in her heart, and laughter on her lips. She had an impish sense of humour. Her colleague, Suzette, was two days older than she, so Hannah always insisted that Suzette should buy all the rail tickets, etc., because of her great seniority!

One day they were asked to conduct a meeting at Meath Place, a Quaker work set in a less affluent area of Dublin. On the way, the two ladies had tea, and Hannah contrived to spill some down her dress. Once at the meeting, Suzette started speaking about being 'whiter than snow', and the pair of them suddenly realised the funny side of it. They had immense difficulty suppressing their giggles.

As a girl, Hannah had wanted for nothing. But now she was compelled to live in a cramped caravan and make do with whatever was available. She was once on a cycle team of two with only one machine between them! So one of them would ride the cycle a certain distance before walking on. Then, when the other person reached the bike, which had been parked in a hedge or ditch, she would jump on and ride off until she caught up the walker. Then they'd change over!

But there was one practical skill Hannah never quite managed to master. It has to be said that she lacked any calling to become a cook! At home, there had been servants to look after that sort of thing; while at Bible College, like most students at that time, she was too busy studying to get involved in practising the culinary arts.

One of her partners in FEB refused to accept Hannah's usual excuses for not slaving over a hot oven, and insisted that she should take her turn. But as it resulted in her becoming a martyr to indigestion on those days when Hannah cooked, the plan clearly failed to work! In the end, Hannah was paired up with a lady worker who was almost as incompetent as she. However, the villagers soon sized up the situation and took pity on the famished evangelists, either by taking them into their own homes for meals, or by going round to the caravan to do the cooking!

If anyone had told her then that one day she would become housekeeper for a hospital, Hannah would have sent for the smelling salts. The whole idea was as improbable as it was undesirable!

III

The Friends Evangelistic Band was interdenominational from the outset. But the Quaker influence remained strong; particularly the practice of waiting on God in silence.

So every morning, after cleaning up their small caravan, Hannah and her companion would begin the day, Quaker fashion, sitting in quietness, free from any hype or undue excitement, simply seeking to realise the Presence. Then they would pray together, as though holding a conversation with Him (*The Hearing Heart*, p 38).

Sometimes the fire would kindle in their hearts. Then words would flow, joy would bubble up into song, and their spirits would dance like David before the Ark. Two ladies who knew Hannah well, say they would find it hard to close their eyes when she prayed, as they were transfixed by her shining face.

But there would also be times of deep humbling. Living in the close confines of a caravan, could cause tensions to arise between the workers. It also revealed every quirk of character. There was no hiding place.

Hannah still had plenty of rough edges to be smoothed away. One of her two sisters, Ruth and Naomi, had bridled when Hannah witnessed to her on one occasion. 'It's people like you who put me off being a Christian,' she had replied. 'You may be happier in yourself. But so far as I can see, you are no less selfish than you were before, and you still want all your own way' (*The Hearing Heart*, p 33). It was a salutary reminder to her that the old Hannah did not disappear overnight after her life-changing experience at Keswick. So now, in the goldfish bowl of a caravan, all her character defects were exposed. Hence confession was the order of the day. Forgiveness needed to be sought and given if their prayers were to remain unhindered.

Then too, they needed to spread their material needs before the Lord in prayer. Hannah's father was wealthy. But like the rest of the Band, she looked to God alone for the supply of all her needs. It was a principle of FEB that no appeal for money should ever be made. So there were times when the workers had to live on prayer and fresh air!

This was a whole new world for Hannah, and it opened her eyes to the miracle of God's supply. *The Hearing Heart* selects one story in particular to show how Hannah's faith, or lack of it, was rebuked and how prayer was wonderfully answered.

The two roomed cottage in which she and her companion were being housed at one time, was faced with a crisis when the store of coal ran out during a miners' strike. The hosts had a sick cow that needed treatment requiring hot water. They also had a family and two guests who needed food and warmth.

So they took to prayer in a big way. Hannah said 'Amen' very loudly to cover up her feelings of unbelief. But an hour or two later, the ladies came down from the loft, wrapped in warm blankets, to find a coal cart trundling up the rutted track to deliver a totally unexpected consignment of the precious fuel.

It appeared that some coal trucks had belatedly arrived at the railway sidings in Ludlow the day before, and the host's name was at the top of the list. In no time at all, the dying fire was revived, the kettle boiled, the cow treated, and the household fed.

If that had been a wholly exceptional experience, it could have been put down to 'coincidence'. But as Archbishop William Temple wryly observed, it is a striking coincidence that coincidences always seem to happen when we pray!

It was also through these unhurried times of quiet waiting on God, that guidance was so often given or checked out. The Quakers spoke much about 'the bidding of the Spirit': that inner nudge, which indicated that the pillar of cloud and fire was moving on, or that some cherished plan needed to be either amended or revoked. Significantly, Hannah called her life story, *The Hearing Heart*.

As she pointed out in that narrative, some Christians are not impressed by talk about 'guidance' because they prefer to make decisions based on common sense. The thought of divine leading seems too 'mystical' for their more down-to-earth approach. On the other hand, there are some who imagine that almost any and every odd happening or inner impulse is of God, and can charge along a given course of action without pausing to seek confirmation from God.

In her most winsome account of FEB, Bessie Bryers,

widow of a former General Secretary, quotes from Thomas Cook of Cliff College, on this whole question of seeking God's will:

> Divine impressions come gently, and the more they are prayed about, the stronger they become. Other impressions come with a rush, and fade away when we wait before God to know His will. No impression is from God if it would lead us to act contrary to the teaching of Scripture or against enlightened reason or our sense of right (p 39).

All this calls for a child-like heart, ever open to the Spirit of God, and willing to be ruthlessly honest with oneself. 'It requires discipline too,' Hannah wrote. There must be 'no indulging in delightful daydreams about ourselves.' So it means guarding the mind against invading fears, or pleasures, or cares: a willingness to be open with other people, and an 'unresentful acceptance' of their reminder that we may not always be right, but that in fact we are quite often wrong!

7 Those Two Veiled Guides

I

The *Friends Witness* for February 1929 announced that Miss Hannah Hurnard of FEB was visiting Palestine and Syria that month. In fact, she and her brother Robert Bracy, always known as Bracy, were accompanying their father on a fact-finding tour of the Middle East.

Samuel took a vital interest in the plight of the Armenians living in Syria. He gave lavishly to help set up employment projects for many of the 150,000 refugees there, and used the columns of the *Friends Witness* to appeal for help. Armenia had been the first known 'Christian' nation in history. Now its people were being decimated by Turkish massacres.

In addition, Samuel was deep into biblical prophecy. Nine years previously he had published his little paperback studies on the Book of Revelation. In 1930, a new, enlarged, hard-backed version of the book was to be published. Hence the Palestine end of his tour was of special interest. It gave him the chance to bone up on all the developments that had taken place in the twenty-two years since he had last visited the area.

Samuel was hugely impressed. At Haifa, a new township, plus a magnificent Technical College, won his admiration. He enjoyed strolling along the wide boulevards of the modern city of Tel Aviv. In Jerusalem, he was impressed by the Hebrew University. Out in the countryside, he investigated programmes for reclaiming land, planting forests, establishing kibbutzim and developing education.

Nowadays, we take all these, and other spectacular advances in the relatively young State of Israel, for granted. We also appreciate the political problems posed by mass immigration and national expansion. But for Samuel, with his strongly biblical orientation, such events were profoundly significant. He recalled God's promises to regather His sons from near and far (Jer 31:8,10; Isa 43:5,6). And he maintained that they were living in what he called 'These Transition Years', similar to the time of transition 'while the ark was a preparing' (1 Peter 3:20, KJV; Matt 24:37). His article on the subject published in the March issue of the *Friends Witness* while he was still in Palestine, sets out any number of firmly-held convictions about Israel's future in the land, including the rebuilding of the Temple.

But while Hannah and Bracy loved the sights and scenes associated with the story of Jesus, they were bored stiff by Zionism, and in Hannah's case, felt no particular liking for the Jewish people. So while their father explored projects and devoured statistics, Hannah and Bracy bathed in the warm waters of the Mediterranean, or revelled in the lovely hills round Galilee.

II

Once back from exotic cities like Aleppo and Jerusalem, Hannah was soon hard at work in the depths of rural England. But in April the following year, she was given a new role. Such was the development of FEB's work throughout the country, that it was becoming necessary to appoint a Deputation worker, and Hannah seemed the ideal choice.

Thereafter, her name rarely appeared in the columns of the *Friends Witness*. Deputation work is rarely glamorous! But Hannah herself was enjoying life in FEB as much as ever. 'I was extraordinarily happy in the Band and could not help hoping that I would be allowed to work there for some time to come,' she wrote in her life story (p 48).

But she had already discovered since leaving for the High Places with her Shepherd Lover, that her guides were to be those two veiled figures: Suffering and Sorrow.

During her first year in training at Ridgelands Bible College, just when she was experiencing all the joy of being freed from a lifelong handicap, Hannah was suddenly summoned back to Hill House where her lovely fifty-five year old mother lay dying.

It had been a comfort to Hannah that whenever her mother had cancelled a speaking appointment during that last year of her life, she had been able to say 'but my daughter Hannah will come in my place.' Rose herself had rejoiced over and over again that her deeply unhappy daughter had found peace of heart at last.

The parting had not been easy, especially as Grandmother Densham had assumed, rather too readily, that the quiet little Hannah was the ideal daughter to care for Samuel when Rose finally slipped away from them. Only the intervention of Rose herself spared Hannah from making an inescapable commitment under pressure from Grandmother. 'I thought thou felt that the Lord was calling thee to be a missionary!' the dying woman had said to her distraught daughter. 'I do, I do,' she'd said so feelingly. 'Then do His will whatever happens,' Rose whispered. 'Father wants that too.'

Five years after that sad day in June 1925 when mother and daughter had bidden each other farewell, Hannah found herself in Ireland as Deputation Secretary of the Friends Evangelistic Band. Suddenly, she was confronted once more with her original vow to serve as a missionary.

Hannah's account of the episode describes a works' outing to 'Ireland's Eye', a famous beauty spot near Dublin, where, after leaving the factory girls behind, she climbed a nearby height alone. She became conscious that the Lord Himself was speaking to her about her call to the mission field. As she read Daniel 9, and reflected on the way in which the prophet had identified himself with the Jewish people, it came as a shock to realise that she too was being asked to get along-side God's covenant people, the Jews.

A call like that rarely happens in a vacuum, of course. She had visited the Holy Land less than two years previously. The emphasis at Keswick Convention on the gospel being 'to the Jew first' could not have escaped her attention. Also her father's teaching about the place of Israel in God's unfolding purposes, must have affected her. Most months the *Friends Witness*, which he co-edited, contained reports, expositions, and challenges about events in Palestine.

So it is not entirely surprising that this sensitive student of Scripture, with a soul so responsive to the Spirit's prompt-ings, should have felt the call so clearly. Moreover, the inner awareness that deep changes were about to happen in her personal life, meant that she was open to whatever He might say to her.

Thus the rocks against which she leant that day at Ireland's Eye, became the altar on which she gave herself afresh to the Shepherd Lover who had called her to the High Places.

But what made the scene so poignant was the realisation that she would be exchanging the warm companionship of the Band for life among people she found it difficult to like, let alone love. Moreover, having lost her mother just when they had become drawn so closely together through their shared love of the Lord Jesus, she was now confronted with the trauma of leaving behind a widowed father whom she dearly loved.

Yet again she discovered that each milestone in her pil-grimage was a tombstone too. What she was not to know until later was that her mother had once longed to serve among Jewish people herself, and that Hannah had been ded-icated while still in the womb, to go in her place.

III

Every call has to be tested if it is not to evaporate as soon as the fires of trial hot up. And Hannah's was no exception.

It proved difficult for her to convince her room-mate that God had called her to Palestine. 'How can you be so sure?' she had rightly insisted. As for the leaders of FEB, they were more than dubious. The need in Britain as a whole presented a mission field wide enough for even the most intrepid missionary. Why go to Palestine of all places? The fact that God was blessing her work in FEB should surely give her pause to think again.

But at least her father approved. It had been her mother's dying wish that Hannah should serve as a missionary overseas, while Samuel could not have imagined a joy greater than having a daughter privileged to work among God's people, Israel. 'How can I ever bless the Lord sufficiently for such parents as mine?' she wrote in *The Hearing Heart*. 'How can I ever express the debt I owe to them?' (p 53).

So she applied to the British Jews Society (BJS), the Free Church equivalent of the Anglican organisation, The Church's Ministry among Jewish people (CMJ), which had pioneered Protestant work in Palestine a century earlier.

However, like many another candidate, equally convinced of a call to serve in a particular field, Hannah found her application rebuffed. BJS pointed out that since Hannah was not trained as either a secretary, teacher or nurse, she lacked the kind of qualifications needed for their work in Haifa. There was certainly no room in their ranks for a lady evangelist, especially as Orthodox Jews do not take kindly to being taught by a woman! But they added that Dr James Churcher, who supervised the work at Haifa, was due in England within a few months and that if Hannah still felt sure of God's call, he would be glad to meet with her.

IV

By now, Hannah's certainty had deepened into a desire that could not be denied. Yet when the long-awaited interview with Dr Churcher eventually took place, her hopes were to nose-dive yet again.

This time, the problem was her health. The hot and humid atmosphere of Haifa was not conducive to a highly-strung temperament like Hannah's. She was certainly not robust. A short stay might be feasible. But any long term residency seemed out of the question, unless she was willing to leave her bones in Palestine. 'Why not think about serving among Jewish people in London or Cairo?' Dr Churcher suggested.

One would have thought that the dust and dirt of Egypt was every bit as trying as the heat and humidity of Haifa! In any case, it had been 'Palestine' and not Cairo, that had fastened itself on her heart up at Ireland's Eye.

But to her credit, Hannah was willing to check it out. And when she opened her Bible at Exodus 3:10, and read: 'Come now and I will send thee to...Egypt', it looked as though there might be something in the doctor's suggestion after all! However, a moment's reflection on that particular verse might have shown that God's command to Moses was in fact designed to lead him OUT of Egypt!

Eventually Hannah concluded that there had been such peace in her heart about going to Palestine, she should persist with her application, even though she felt no great drawing towards the Jewish people there, quite the reverse. In the end the Mission agreed that she should go to Haifa at her own expense, and serve there in a stop-gap capacity for a trial period. 'How deeply thankful I was to the Mission...for the loving, patient way they accepted me,' Hannah later wrote.

Friends from near and far gathered for her valedictory service at Lexden Village Hall on Monday evening, January 11th, 1932. Frank Exley, Secretary of the British Jews Society, spoke of new opportunities opening up in Haifa. May Cheal sang a solo and John Reid, Superintendent of the Railway Mission, spoke about Acts 11:12. Then, after he had sung the old gospel hymn: 'Anywhere with Jesus I can safely go', Hannah addressed the meeting, using the words of Psalm 116:16 as her text:

> O Lord, truly I am your servant,
> I am your servant, the son of your maidservant;
> You have freed me from my chains.

'The meeting was singularly impressive throughout, with a great stillness,' the *Friends Witness* reported. Certainly the final hymn could not have been more appropriate for the former Miss Much-Afraid, as she set out with her Shepherd for the uplands of discipleship more than 2,500 miles from home:

> My goal is God Himself, not joy, nor peace,
> Not even blessing, but Himself, my God,
> 'Tis His to lead me there, not mine, but His –
> At any cost, dear Lord, by any road.

> One thing I know, I cannot say Him nay;
> One thing I do, I press towards my Lord:
> My God my glory here from day to day,
> And in the glory there my great reward.

8 *A Stop-gap in Haifa*

I

Hannah wrote home unfailingly every week of her life in Palestine, and Samuel always took time out to reply to her. After his death in 1949, Hannah's step-mother kept up the correspondence.

The letters themselves have long since been consigned to oblivion. But Samuel sometimes quoted from them in the columns of the *Friends Witness*, which he helped to edit. These precious paragraphs reflected the wide-eyed wonder Hannah felt at the privilege of being a 'missionary', and the joy of living in the land which Jesus loved. They also revealed that flair for writing which would find full flower twenty years later in the books she then began to pen.

Nowadays, no worker among Jewish people would want to use the title 'missionary', which is so offensive to Jewish people. Enormous damage has been inflicted on them by enforced conversions, and by the Church's anathema on the Synagogue. But Hannah had no such hang-ups about the word at that time. She had been 'sent out' to be an evangelist: seeking 'the lost sheep of the House of Israel'.

So, as she wrote during the out-bound voyage:

> There are fourteen missionaries on board – six at my table. They are all going to India. Four of us at the table are young, and going out for the first time. The weather has been simply perfect, and the sea like glass and the sun gorgeous. It is too funny in the evenings to see Dr H having a Tamil lesson at

> one table, Drs A and S learning Urdoo (sic) at another, and myself deep in Hebrew. The passengers say that every other person you speak to on the boat is a missionary or a Scotchman (sic)!

As always, Hannah revelled in the power and splendour of nature:

> Yesterday we passed Stromboli. It was simply belching out smoke, and we passed so close you could see the people on the island. Fancy building little towns at the foot of a volcano! Every now and then we saw quite a red glow, but there was no lava sizzling into the sea, as there is sometimes.

So they sailed via the toe of Italy and across to Port Said. Dr Churcher must have been prescient, for here she was berthing in Egypt! A member of the Mission staff met her off the boat, helped her over a number of problems with the Customs, and travelled with her by train to Haifa.

Hannah's father had taken special interest in the developing rail system which linked Palestine with neighbouring countries, seeing in it a fulfilment of Isaiah 19:23: 'In that day there will be a highway from Egypt to Assyria...In that day Israel will be a third along with Egypt and Assyria, a blessing on the earth.'

He wasn't to know that the rail network would shrink – although there are currently plans for the French to revitalise Israel's railways! But there are busy roads and throbbing flightpaths instead, and political agreements to facilitate travel in that part of the world, at least for the time being.

II

Hannah was glad to settle into the Mission compound after her long train journey across the north of Sinai and up by the Palestinian seaboard to Haifa. She also expressed appreciation for the heart-warming fellowship she had experienced en route:

'Isn't it just lovely of the Lord to have given me those happy times on the boat, and so many nice new friends?', she wrote.

In no time at all she felt at home with the two German sisters who worked in Dr Churcher's clinic and was trying out her embryonic German on them!

> It is simply marvellous how my German has sprouted. I can understand whole sermons quite easily and talk quite freely, but, of course, incorrectly. The two sisters...are very kind indeed.

The weather that winter was decidedly chilly with record falls of snow and some quite blustery conditions. But when the sun shone, her heart rejoiced at 'the splendours of Carmel and Sharon'.

> Haifa is in the middle of the rainy season now, and is belching (squelching?) with mud. But when it is not raining, the sun is simply glorious. I did not remember the views were so lovely. By climbing the garden wall high up on the hill, you get right out on to Carmel itself, with no houses anywhere – just trees and shrubs and wild flowers. From my windows, on a clear day, I can see Mt Hermon very, very plainly, with the most wonderfully coloured mountains and the bay in the foreground. I am very happy indeed, and it is so lovely to be able to work right away.

The clinic was always busy.

> There is a great deal of sickness and influenza at present, and the Medical Mission is crowded. I help there three mornings in the week, the idea being to take Miss Churcher's place when she goes on furlough (vacation), but whether this sanguine hope will ever be realised, I greatly doubt. Do pray I shall really get on with the medical work, and not be the complete duffer I am at present. They do need extra help badly. About sixty to ninety dressings a day is a lot for one or two nurses.

Eventually she was to chafe against the stale sermons

served up by the aged Minister at Sunday services. But in those first few weeks in Haifa, Hannah was brimming with enthusiasm.

> The tourist boats are arriving now (she wrote on March 1st) and we had quite a number of visitors at the meetings on Sunday, and twenty of us sat down to tea in Mrs Rohold's drawing room afterwards...I love Sundays here. The meetings are all in English, and are very helpful.

III

In February of that first year in Palestine, Hannah attended a crowded meeting held to celebrate the life and ministry of Mrs Rohold's late husband, who had died just one year before at the age of fifty-five.

He had been born in Jerusalem, the son of a Rabbi, and brought up as an Orthodox Jew, spending much time studying the Talmud. But one day, he met a couple of CMJ workers near the Garden of Gethsemane, and he was so impressed by them, that he took and read the New Testament they'd proffered him. As a result, he began to pay secret visits to their home. At last, he could no longer keep quiet about his faith in Jesus as Messiah.

But he knew it would mean total upheaval in his home. A friend of his who had taken the same spiritual journey was in fact almost killed by his fanatical family. So S.B. Rohold travelled to Britain and lived for a while in London. After studying at the Glasgow Bible Institute he was put in charge of the Bonar Memorial Mission in the city.

He attended the famous World Missionary Conference at Edinburgh in 1910, as one of only two Hebrew Christian delegates. Then he went to Toronto, where he established the first Hebrew Christian Synagogue (Messianic Assembly). He also served as President of the Hebrew Christian Alliance which he had helped to form.

In 1919, he returned to Palestine, where he became Principal of the Mount Carmel Bible School in Haifa, and

Head of the Mission where Hannah now served. He had in fact died while on a visit to Cairo.

Already Hannah was walking in the shadow of great pilgrims. Much of her journey was to be 'on the shores of loneliness'. But as she looked around at the thirty or so people in Mrs Rohold's room that afternoon, and reflected on all she had heard of this great Jewish teacher and leader, she realised afresh that there was a whole host of witnesses inspiring her to run with endurance the race that was set before her.

After a visit to Beirut, Hannah returned to Haifa as one of thirty-nine workers from nineteen different nationalities attending the Missionary Conference on Carmel in late April. She wrote of the night they arrived at Karmel Heim, 'with Haifa looking rather like a shining town far below, and the most lovely reflections from the lights of ships just inside the harbour.' She recalled the words of Mr Maxwell, from CMJ's centre in Jerusalem, as he spoke on Mark 3:14, 'that they might be with Him', and urged each worker to seek 'a deeper intimacy with the Lord Jesus'. That evening, the meeting closed with all the missionaries unitedly praying the Lord's Prayer in their respective languages.

IV

Hannah was a stop-gap teacher as well as a stop-gap nurse. And clearly the Jewish children then were little different from the lively young harum-scarums in Israel now!

> My classes are a great joy. I have two every Monday, Tuesday, Wednesday and Thursday. The first at 4.30 p.m. is for Hebrew children. I have to teach them English, and they know none at all, not even German, as all adult Jews do. The difficulty of interesting about twelve of the naughtiest little children in the world in the English language, without a common language, must be experienced to be realised. The other workers say it will help my Hebrew, but I notice that none of them offer to do it themselves! Jewish children are very undisciplined. However, the Lord does help wonderfully.

The next class from about 5.30 – 7 p.m. is a splendid opportunity. I have five young Jews and one Jewess. They know a certain amount of English, and we always study the Bible. At first they were unwilling for this; now they are much keener, and ask questions and we discuss what we read and write, and then they re-write the whole lesson for me again when they go home. On Saturday I have a nice Bible class for educated Jewish girls, and on Sunday afternoon another one for big Arab girls.

However, by June 27th, Hannah was feeling frustrated at being just a 'stop-gap'.

The clinic gets bigger and bigger. I simply don't know how the doctor and sisters keep at it day after day, especially with lots of outside cases too. I only go on the lightest days in the week, and have no outside cases at all. It makes me feel terribly ashamed to see how hard others work, and how little I can do. I do enjoy everything tremendously, and long for the time when I shall be really 'worked in' and feel I am of some use. The girls in the Bible class are rather a problem just at present. I think their friends and families are beginning to want to move them from Christian influence. The week before last they were saying that it didn't seem likely there was anything after death...There seems an awful lot of Modernism, even among Jews...This afternoon Miss Churcher and I had tea with my Hebrew teacher in her home. They chatted away together in Hebrew at a tremendous rate, and I could hardly follow it at all. How lovely it will be when I can really speak Hebrew!!

But there were signs of success in her teaching from time to time.

The evening class grows bigger and bigger. I have got very fond of my pupils. They are very keen to learn now and are much easier to handle, and behave well. But alas! although they will talk freely about spiritual things, they will not believe. They generally end up by saying: 'Yes, Jesus was a good man, and it is interesting to read about Him, but I don't believe in Him.'

Last Tuesday Mrs ben Maier took charge of my babies, and I went into the bigger Children's Meeting and took my turn at speaking to them. It all had to be translated into Arabic, and it is very different speaking and telling a story through an interpreter. Our Arab worker takes these children, and he can make them listen and he interprets well. But oh! to be able to get hold of the language!

Her letters home also speak of times when she could seek recreation and renewal in the unspoilt beauty of her surroundings.

The other morning (she wrote on July 3rd) I saw a large green frog-like creature, with a long lizard tail and yellow spots, blinking at me from a small tree outside my window. It might be a chameleon. The woodpeckers make a great show here. They are light green birds, with red heads and yellow underneaths. I love lying on Carmel and watching the hawks. Everything is much dried up, but Carmel keeps beautiful in spite of it.

V

During the summer, Hannah was taken ill, and needed treatment at Nazareth Hospital. But a holiday down south with Sister Caroline and Dr Churcher renewed her health and vigour.

She loved the silent and desolate Judean desert.

It was perfectly wonderful – not a tree or shrub anywhere, only yellow-red sand and rocks, and the hills piled on top of each other.

Riding a donkey along the dried up wadis and over trackless hills under a blazing sun, was an unforgettable experience for Hannah. Caroline's animal pitched her over its head on one occasion. 'But my donkey was remarkably surefooted,' Hannah wrote. 'It never slipped once. But it had a mania for showing how well it could go downhill!'

They reached the women's tower in a monastery late one afternoon, and after drawing water from the well in the floor, brewed tea and coffee. After supper they watched the moon rise over the desert.

It was a wonderful sight. A fiery moon suddenly rose out of a rose-pink haze over the mountains of Moab, and the whole desert turned pink. Then quite suddenly it was night, and the hills turned silver white in the moonlight, as though they were covered by snow.

They bathed in the sea at Tel Aviv one day, and on another occasion, rode by donkey from Bethlehem to the caves of Adullam, where the girls slipped out of their dresses and donned overalls so they could crawl through the caves and crevices in the labyrinth of tunnels there.

Late in the afternoon, they gradually emerged from the silent emptiness of the desert, to find, first a wall, then an olive tree, and eventually a human habitation. It was dark by the time they rode, like Joseph and Mary, into the little town of Bethlehem.

9 *Detour through the Desert*

On January 21st, 1933, Hannah spent the first anniversary of her arrival in Palestine, walking the dogs on Carmel, and picking some cyclamen to put into a pretty vase she had received as a Christmas present, before writing home.

She could look back on a fascinating year, full of new experiences. Quite obviously she was frustrated at being an odd-job person, still struggling to find her role and to learn the language(s). But she had witnessed to the gospel among patients at the clinic, and taught English at evening classes. In fact the classes were going well. 'The pupils are so nice and so interested, and I get extremely fond of them, especially the ones who were extra difficult when they first came,' she wrote that day.

It is a tribute to the work of the Mission that local Jewish leaders set up a medical clinic almost next door, and held evening classes to coincide with Hannah's. They would hardly have wanted to set up in rivalry to an outfit that was ineffective! Some of the patients and students went along to see what these new facilities were like. But they soon came back to the Mission.

A week later, on January 27th, Hannah wrote home again. The bad news was that their best donkey had been stolen, so everyone was upset. The loss also made it difficult to transport food and goods from the town. The good news was that a Jewish lad, summoned back to Poland on a ruse, cast off by his family for declaring himself a 'Christian', and then reported to the Military who promptly demanded that he finish his eighteen months in the army, suddenly rang up from Haifa Harbour while Mrs Rohold and Hannah were enjoying a mid-afternoon cup of tea! Their prayers had been answered. The boy had been able to escape from Poland and make his way back to Palestine.

Two months later, Samuel Hurnard made his third visit to the Holy Land, and was able to take part in a staff coach outing to Mount Tabor organised by his daughter Hannah.

Needless to say, he was soon off on his travels, his eagle eye taking in all that was happening. He noted how Jewish tractors and primitive Arab ploughs cultivated neighbouring plots. After a very dry winter, which left even the lowland wells empty, he was glad to welcome some showers. 'The latter rains bring gold,' the Arabs say. In Jerusalem, cars and camels jostled in the narrow streets. Out in the kibbutzim, irreligion abounded. Among Christians, 'worldliness, superstition, hereditary bias, unbelief and division' saddened Samuel. But he was pleased that the sales of Bibles were up.

Hannah spent her annual leave among friends and family in England that summer. But she was glad to get back to Haifa in October. There was no more talk about her stay being temporary! However, before the month was over, Arab riots broke out in the city, and two people were shot dead outside the clinic.

Hitler had become Chancellor of Germany on January 30th. Already Concentration Camps were being set up on the Continent, so Jewish people were escaping to Palestine wherever possible, and the Arab population was quite literally up in arms over this influx of European Jews. One day Mrs Rohold, armed only with a smile, braved a mob brandishing sticks. There was a curfew each night from 6 p.m. to 5 a.m. On November 4th, the Arabs went on strike. Ugly crowds refused to disperse when ordered to do so, and shot at the police when they charged. The uprising was eventually quelled, but at a price.

II

In the spring of 1934, Hannah joined a group of workers from Tiberias on a visit to six of the kibbutzim in the Jordan valley. It was lovely to be away from the tense atmosphere of Haifa, and to enjoy seeing fields of purple, mauve, white and scarlet anemones with tufts of flowers that looked like yellow lilies. The whole valley was a patchwork of land, with cattle wading knee-deep in corn, and workers tending dark-coloured strips of ploughed land.

They were impressed by all they saw on the settlements, nodding their heads sagely when examining the cattle, cooing over new-born lambs, and admiring the incubator with its 10,000 eggs. Hannah was pleased to discover how her limited Hebrew softened hearts and opened doors.

She sensed an air of disillusionment among the kibbutzniks. For a while they had been engrossed in pioneer work like children with a new toy. But the novelty had begun to wear off. She talked to one sullen girl who had been in a particular kibbutz for fourteen years, and 'got a very strong feeling that in the course of those years the new toy had got broken and no longer appealed.'

'The people in these colonies openly scoffed at the very idea of God,' she wrote in a letter home. Many were indignant that their visitors should try to leave literature at their kibbutz. When Hannah mentioned the Messiah to the sullen girl, she had said, 'There is no Messiah and I have no hope.' Hannah's reply was what one would expect of an eager young evangelist. 'I don't think I could bear life if I had no hope and no faith in God,' she said. 'I have a hunger in my heart which only He has been able to satisfy.' But the girl simply shrugged her shoulders and moved off to speak to the men.

Hannah was able to enjoy a rest day at Tabgha with her

friends, away from the suffocating godlessness of the settlements. They strolled through the banana plantation, gazed at
shoals of fish and mini water tortoises in the Galilee, and
sheltered by a pool overhung with eucalyptus trees. All her
love of nature spilled over into her letter home.

> Here the herdsmen had brought their flocks and herds of
> goats, and the cows had waded out into the cool water
> almost up to their necks, while the sheep and goats were
> lying at the edge. It reminded us very much of the 23rd Psalm.
> Here we spent the rest of the morning and afternoon bathing
> or lying about in the shade watching the kingfishers, in their
> vivid blue and red, flashing over the water. The real country,
> off the main roads and away from the towns, is fascinating,
> and I do wonder why unfortunate tourists are hounded from
> place to place looking at ugly buildings on improbable sites.

III

There was much to encourage Hannah and her fellow workers in the Medical and Evangelistic Centre at Haifa. They
were having to look for a larger property because their
own had been outgrown. A Christmas party held for Jewish
believers, attracted some other Jews as well.

The winter was more severe than usual, with frequent
cloudbursts over Haifa. Nazareth had 18.5 inches of rain by
the end of January. But hard winters meant full cisterns, and
promised good crops.

A.T. Upson of the Nile Mission Press, a leading Arabic
scholar from Hannah's home county of Essex, was welcomed
to Karmel-Heim that spring. Local believers and Christian
workers trekked up to the German rest-home set in pine
forests above Haifa, and were blessed by the chalk-talks for
which this tall, gracious, profoundly deaf missionary states-
man was famous.

In July, Hannah wrote home to say that she had been 'liberated' to spend the month at Jerusalem studying Hebrew. In
the event, she stayed two whole months, sharing a room
with her Finnish friend, Miss Havas, a student at the Hebrew

University. Another student gave Hannah Hebrew lessons every morning.

Their's was open house, and any number of Jewish students, doctors, nurses and shop-workers dropped in: some Orthodox, others less so. 'I don't believe there was one who came in, not a single one, without having heard of Jesus Christ,' she wrote.

Back in Haifa her Bible class had been decidedly fractious: 'very wild and difficult,' is how she put it. But those eight weeks spent in Jerusalem, with lively students expressing an interest in Hannah's faith, proved an oasis. 'I think it was the happiest two months that I have had in Palestine,' she said.

This 'simply marvellous' experience inspired her to develop a similar outreach among Jewish people once she got back to Haifa. 'Do tell me how I can get in touch with people in Haifa as you have done in Jerusalem,' she said to Miss Havas. The reply took her aback. 'Give up teaching them,' she was told. 'Go and learn among them: join their evening classes.'

'So I followed this advice,' Hannah later wrote, 'and instead of sitting at the head of the table teaching three or four, I sat in a classroom with thirty others, all of them Jews or Jewesses learning Hebrew, and it seemed to me that every one of them was interested in me, and anxious to show me kindness.'

IV

Hannah was beginning to develop her own distinctive ministry. But the four years' apprenticeship she had served in the land, had not been easy. She had suffered the culture shock of leaving an affluent life in the West, for a much more primitive lifestyle in an Eastern environment. The damp, enervating climate at Haifa was very trying too, as Dr Churcher had said it would be. After a day spent working in the clinic and teaching at evening classes, she would sometimes weep with sheer tiredness while undressing and getting ready for bed.

Sleep was not always easy when the nights were hot and sticky. Then at 4 or 4.30 in the morning, she would haul herself out of bed, ready to start another day of busy activity.

Keswick had taught her the vital importance of 'the morning watch'. But quite apart from the fact that the spiritual atmosphere of the Holy Land is often inimical to prayer, she was simply exhausted. So she often felt unsettled, restless, and tense.

Nor was it easy for Hannah to find herself a mere 'junior' at the Centre, when she had been an influential figure in the Friends Evangelistic Band. She lacked the skills, experience and linguistic ability her colleagues possessed. So there were times when she felt decidedly redundant!

It would have helped if the Sunday ministry had been fresh and invigorating. But the ageing Minister often served up stale fare. Moreover the weekly staff prayer meeting seemed stilted and formal, in comparison with the warm spontaneity of prayer times in FEB. The leaders frowned on any effusiveness in worship, regarding such emotional warmth as demonstrating an over-familiarity with the Almighty. As for Hannah's desire to have one special prayer partner, that was likely to lead to 'cliquishness'. So she had to accept the discipline of submissiveness: which was not always easy for one whom a male colleague once described as 'the proud Miss Hannah'!

It is to her credit that she came to realise the wisdom of her leaders at Haifa. In fact she began to realise that some of her motives were not as spiritual as she thought! One reason for wanting a special prayer partner, for instance, was that it gave her the chance to 'pray about' the very evident defects in her colleagues which she had been swift to discern, and which she believed would be a cause of stumbling to others! It was all totally sincere, of course. As she said in her second autobiography, *The Opened Understanding*, privately published in 1958, 'I had never even suspected that under the guise of praying for others, I was actually criticising them and joining the great adversary in his condemnation of them' (p 90).

Yet, in spite of all the battles Hannah fought in those early years, she discovered much delight in God. The 'irresistible joy and lightheartedness of the former years' may have subsided. But the very difficulties she faced forced her to 'thrust deeper into the river of His love and grace'. They were in fact very happy years.

Then in 1936 came the crisis in Hannah's life which resulted in a most surprising and creative adventure for God.

10   *The Valley of Buds and Fruits*

F ollowing her two months in Jerusalem learning Hebrew during the summer of 1935, Hannah had stopped off in Switzerland to polish up her German, and then taken her annual vacation in England.

But she could not wait to get back to Haifa so she could implement the advice her friend Miss Havas had given. Both on the train journey across France, and on the boat to Port Said, she teamed up with friends from Ridgelands days. The weather was perfect, and the sea calm. Once in Haifa, even the dogs were glad to welcome her back!

By November 17th she had found an ideal little room in the Jewish quarter, and moved in. She was blessed with the services of a good Jewish cook, 'who charges very reasonably', as Hannah put it.

Each morning Hannah would sit on the balcony eating breakfast, and looking at the sun rising over the hills which enclose the Jordan valley. On November 21st she held a flat-warming party for six friends. Apart from Sundays, which she spent at the compound, Hannah welcomed visitors to tea almost every day.

Up at Ireland's Eye, she had admitted no great love for Jewish people. But she had the wisdom to know, that provided she was willing to accept God's plan, she would be enabled to identify with them. And so it proved. During the curfews in Haifa, she had wandered down to the Jewish quarter to take English lessons, since Jewish people were not allowed to go up to the Centre, and Arab boys had taunted her for being a 'Jewess'. Now she was actually living in the Jewish quarter and welcoming her new neighbours to tea.

The room was ideal from every point of view. It was close to the Reading Room where she still held some lessons, and also within walking distance of the Technicum where she had Hebrew evening classes. So it saved on bus fares. For most of her time in Palestine, Hannah lived on an allowance of £200 per annum.

It ought to have been idyllic, and in many ways it was. But she was involved in a spiritual warfare. 'It is a tremendous fight,' she said in one letter home. 'The enemy seemed to make such an effort to snatch me away, or to depress me in some way.'

Moreover, as Samuel reported in the *Friends Witness* for March 1936, most of the staff at Haifa were ill at one time or another. Dr Churcher had three weeks' sick leave. Then his new wife fell gravely ill. Hannah herself had to spend time in hospital suffering from bronchitis and laryngitis. For ten days she could eat nothing. They feared diphtheria. On January 22nd she was taken back to the compound to recuperate. However, on February 6th, she was able to go back to her own room 'feeling very fit'.

Then came the letter from her father Samuel which proved such a crushing blow to her. He was to marry again.

II

Marjorie Eady was happy at Lexden Village Hall where she'd been converted at the age of ten. She had also become an able Superintendent of the Sunday School there, and as Samuel was a teacher on her staff, they had plenty of opportunity to get better acquainted.

In 1930, Marjorie's mother died. So she cared for her father Frederick. Then, a few years later, Samuel encouraged her to think about spending time at Redcliffe College, of which he was now Chairman. But clearly, Samuel and she had reached an 'understanding', since he made it clear that if ever she were called to serve overseas as a missionary, he would not stand in her way.

So in 1934, Marjorie took a major step in life. Never in her wildest dreams had she imagined herself as a student. Yet here she was, settling into the fellowship of the Bible College in West London under the stern eye of the rather formidable Principal, Miss Miall.

But when it became clear that her place was to be by Samuel's side, and not on any distant shore, Samuel wrote to tell Hannah of their intentions. A fury of resentment filled her heart. She had always been close to him, especially since serving in Palestine. She had cut out a paragraph from one of his letters to her, and kept it in her Bible. 'I want to tell thee my dear daughter, that I count it the greatest privilege of my life to have a daughter as a missionary in the Holy Land and working amongst the Jewish people,' the letter ran. 'I want thee to know what a joy thee has always been to me. There have been times when thee and I have had different opinions on various matters, but I can truly say that in all thy life, thee has never caused me a moment of real sorrow nor anxiety' (sic, *The Opened Understanding*, p 14). Now another person was to be more closely intertwined with Samuel.

Moreover, Marjorie was even younger than Hannah herself! In her second autobiography, Hannah had calculated that there was an eight year gap between them. In fact it was six-and-a-half years. All the same, it was an affront to Hannah's dignity! Small wonder that she felt 'the passion of jealousy and rage' in her heart when her father's letter arrived.

But Marjorie has great strength of character, and so she made up her mind to win over her aggrieved new daughter-in-waiting as soon as it was at all possible. She also has a dry sense of humour! When speaking of her Bible College career, she sometimes says, with a twinkle in her eye, 'I did something far worse than becoming a missionary when I graduated. I married the College Chairman!'

A brief notice in the *Friends Witness* intimated that Marjorie Faith Eady was married to Samuel Fennell Hurnard in Colchester on May 27th, 1936.

III

Meanwhile, severe rioting broke out in Palestine. Indeed the country became well-nigh ungovernable. The Arabs were insisting that all Jewish immigration and land-buying should cease, while the Jews were desperate to escape from the death camps of Germany. Both sides were blaming the British for their plight.

A kibbutz near Mount Tabor was attacked by 300 Arabs, and only the arrival of a British Regiment stationed at Nazareth, prevented a massacre. In Gaza, Arabs cut power supplies and telephone lines. Elsewhere, British residents took refuge in police barracks.

Hannah's letter home on June 22nd, reported that two bombs had been thrown at the corner of her street, but only one person was hurt – the Arab who threw one of the bombs had not run away fast enough. 'However,' she wrote, 'everything goes on much the same as usual, and our work has not been hindered in any way. We are all in good health and happy in the work.' Little Miss Much-Afraid had learned to brave 'the Forests of Danger and Tribulation.'

IV

By the time Hannah left for her annual two month furlough in England, she had started to learn the lesson of renunciation. All around her, battles raged. Within her heart, alien emotions seethed. But during her visit to the Keswick Convention on the way home that July, she resolved to follow *the more excellent way*.

Soon she was climbing the familiar steps up into Hill

House, bowing in Quaker silence before commencing a meal, listening to Samuel's quiet enquiries after her welfare, walking across neatly-clipped lawns and through the colourful gardens of their three-and-a-half acre grounds, feeling the tensions of Palestine slipping away and finding strength to cope with her new situation.

She tells the story humbly and movingly in at least three of her books. In letting go of her hoarded 'rights' and going the extra mile of making things easy for her stepmother, Hannah visibly grew as a Christian. It occurred to her that if there was one thing more embarrassing than having a stepmother six-and-a-half years younger than oneself, it is having a stepdaughter who is six-and-a-half years older!

It also became obvious that Marjorie was able to handle the situation with remarkable maturity, and could wield the weapon of kindness with unerring effectiveness. 'In the end,' Hannah wrote, 'there was no one whom I loved more than my stepmother, and I found that home had become a happier place for me than ever before.'

So Hannah discovered that the way up, is down; that love gains with the giving, and that surrendering one's rights, leads to a deeper experience of God's grace. The lesson was encapsulated in one of her most sensitive little poems:

> Hear the summons night and day
> Calling us to come away.
> From the heights we leap and flow
> To the valleys down below.
> Always answering to the call,
> To the lowest place of all.
> Sweetest urge and sweetest pain,
> To go low and rise again.

V

Back in Haifa, the clinic was busier than ever. New immigrants were crowding into the country, bringing their legacy of much suffering. The war-wounded needed tending, and local people caught up in the riots, had to be treated for trauma, as well as for physical injury.

Hannah was mighty glad that a Hebrew Christian nurse from Germany had been given a permit to join them. Medical work was not Hannah's forte. In the early days she had once taken a swig of clear liquid from a bottle, imagining it to be water, only to end up in hospital being treated for jaundice brought on by swallowing copious quantities of disinfectant.

Hannah was also relieved that someone else could now regulate the crowds in the waiting room! Like most eastern-ers, their patients lacked the stolid Englishman's resignation to the courtesies of queueing, and Hannah never forgot the day she had given a piece of her mind to one particular fel-low who'd muscled ahead of those who had been waiting much longer. It did nothing for her blood pressure that the doctor had actually overruled her! But it says a lot for her genuine humility, that she apologised to the man when he came out of the surgery. To her surprise, the man in turn expressed regret for his behaviour, and explained that his vir-ulent skin condition was sometimes totally unbearable. Even the other patients then softened in their attitude towards him. All the same, Hannah was relieved that this new worker from Dr Francke's Institute in Hamburg could take over her police duties, and keep the peace between these volatile patients!

One day Hannah strolled down to the harbour with a col-league, Miss MacLean, and they went aboard HMS *Valiant.* 'The horrible array of frightful guns of tremendous size and power, with which the whole place bristled, was very dread-ful to a good pacifist like myself,' Hannah wrote.

Up at the Technicum, she joined the special Hebrew classes laid on for the new German Jewish immigrants, and was able to try out her growing facility in both languages.

One evening, the lights failed, and greatly daring, Hannah invited the class and its distinguished teacher to meet in her room nearby.

As they all knew I was a missionary, I never dreamt that they would accept the invitation (she wrote). But they did, and I piloted the whole class to a room dedicated to the service of the Lord Jesus Christ. After that, the class was always held in my room four evenings in the week. I gave them coffee and biscuits, and usually the lessons lasted from 7 to 8.30 or 9.

These young Jews had never read or studied the Old Testament, and after a time they found that I knew it pretty well, so they said to the teacher, 'It won't do that a Gentile should know our Scriptures and we don't. Please let us read a chapter in Hebrew every evening.' Two of the students borrowed my Bibles and took them home.

The teacher was very kind. I was allowed to ask him anything I wanted on Biblical things and Jewish interpretations. He was a real believer in the Bible, and a great lover of the prophecies. He had been in touch with many Christians and even Hebrew Christians, but strongly disapproved of Jews becoming Christians. But a few evenings before I left for England he suddenly said to me, 'In spite of your being a missionary, Miss Hurnard, there is no place in Haifa where I feel so much at home as I do here. I shall miss these evenings very much indeed.' He has now left Haifa (*Friends Witness*, March 1937).

The advice her Finnish friend, Miss Havas, had given her, was bearing fruit. But then came one of those stiff and formal weekly staff prayer meetings at the Centre, which was destined to change the whole direction of Hannah's ministry.

11   *A Baby Austin Motor Car*

Hannah freely admitted that she had been reluctant to start her missionary career in the ranks of FEB. But, on reflection, nothing could have prepared her better for the new adventure awaiting her in Palestine.

To start with, she had learned to live in a horse-drawn trailer caravan, little realising that one day she would drive around Haifa in a vehicle hauled by a horse!

More importantly, life in FEB had schooled her in the work of pioneer evangelism among needy villagers who were often hostile to her message. She had learned to wait on the Holy Spirit for guidance, and to work in tandem with others so that they could reach out to new areas two-by-two, as Jesus instructed.

The new call came to Hannah at one of those stiff and starchy prayer meetings she had often found so unedifying. First there were clinical reports to be shared with the staff as fuel for prayer. Then an Arab evangelist spoke of the visits he and his colleague had made to several Arab villages in the locality, selling Bibles, and gossiping the gospel.

Hannah felt moved to pray with passionate intensity for someone to go out into the new Jewish settlements growing up all around them as well. There were sonorous 'amens' in response to her prayer. But then silence fell! Not that Hannah found that too disconcerting. As a good Quaker, she was used to long empty spaces of quietness. But then, quite unexpectedly, while thinking about the kibbutzim she had visited two years before, Hannah became aware that this was precisely the kind of work she herself was best equipped to undertake.

She did not mention the idea to anyone at this stage, not only because others did not always understand how Hannah could be so confident of having heard 'the still small voice', but also because the whole project would have seemed like moonlight madness. She had no transport or companion, her Hebrew was still weak, and her Arabic was virtually non-existent! In many outlying districts there would have been no accommodation for her. Moreover, many of the new Jewish settlements were violently anti-religious, while those that were religious would not have listened to a woman, least of all one who was English. Was it not the British Mandate which was preventing tens of thousands of Jews from finding sanctuary in Palestine, in spite of the Balfour Declaration signed in November 1917 which promised Jews a homeland there?

Furthermore, rioting was at its height from 1936 onwards, and many of the roads that did exist were mined. Snipers constantly attacked buses and cars.

But when Hannah arrived back in England for an extended stay of three months, her father Samuel warmed to her proposition. He had little imagination, Hannah said, and seemed quite incapable of envisaging any possible dangers there might be. If God had called the dear girl, He could be trusted to take care of her!

Not only did Samuel give her his blessing, he also donated a baby Austin motor car for her use in visiting the villages of Palestine.

II

For the first time since beginning to commute between England and the Holy Land, Hannah was able to sail direct from Southampton to Haifa. 'The weather was horrid,' she wrote. But at least she had plenty of friends on board, and the daily Bible Readings were good. She also had her precious cargo of a baby Austin below decks!

In contrast with her very first visit to Palestine eight years previously, Hannah thought Haifa looked very beautiful as they sailed into its harbour under the bluest skies imaginable. It was wonderful to be back where she now belonged, and to be welcomed so warmly by all and sundry. She was also glad to learn that the new Haifa-Jaffa Highway was to be opened that very day. It meant that all the settlements on the Plain of Sharon were now within visiting distance, and that Jaffa could be reached in an hour and a half, instead of half a day. So her letter was full of praise.

> Now I must tell you about the car. It has been absolutely lovely the way God undertook. My first afternoon back in Haifa I was offered a lift by an Arab Christian friend, who works in the Shipping Agency. He said at once he would get it off the boat and through the Customs. The afternoon the ship arrived he got my car off, paid duty, filled it with petrol, water, and oil, rang me up, met me at the docks and presented the car all ready for me to drive off in. Next morning I got the car tested and registered, number plates made, and every single thing finished, and, would you believe it, the other ten cars from the boat were still standing at the docks unpassed by the Customs!

But the political situation was far from rosy. Three days before her arrival, a hundred Arabs were arrested for killing two British Officials. On October 20th, Jewish immigration was severely cut back to appease Arab militants. Yet attacks continued. The colony at Rosh Pinah in the north, and a bus five miles from Jerusalem in the south, were ambushed. The Haifa-Lydda railway line was blown up. A British military train en route to Egypt was fired on. Four leading Arabs were deported. But the Jewish community protested that preventing their immigrants from landing amounted to religious discrimination.

There was no way that Hannah, or any other English lady,

ought to have ventured out in such conditions. But Hannah
possessed the optimism of faith. After all, God had called her,
new roads were being built by the thousands of new Arab
immigrants being employed by the British, and, as a rule,
women were treated with respect by both Jews and Arabs. In
fact, while no men were given licences to drive around during the troubles, the ban did not apply to women drivers, so
Hannah eventually had carte blanche to travel the roads
unmolested.

III

It so happened that Dr Churcher was away when Hannah
arrived back in Haifa on September 30th, 1937, and this
meant that the nursing sisters were free to accompany her.
Moreover, because the doctor had given the project his blessing, and the sisters shared Hannah's vision, the venture was
virtually up and running straight away.

So on October 14th, just a fortnight after her return, and
six months after her call at the staff prayer meeting in April
1937, Hannah set out in her little baby Austin with Sister
Mercy, alias Sister Caroline from Germany.

Normally the coastal road between Haifa and Acre (Akko)
ran across the sands at low tide, and cars sometimes sank.
But the couple arrived at a German-Jewish settlement mid-
way between the two towns without mishap.

Yet it was a daunting prospect. How could they make contact with total strangers unused to this kind of door-to-door
evangelism? What methods should they use to break down
barriers and to introduce talk about Jesus as Messiah, especially when the Orthodox Jews often spat into the dust and
pronounced a curse on the name Hannah loved more than
any other?

Hannah soon realised that the principles she had imbibed
with FEB were perfectly suited to this new kind of outreach.
They were to seek guidance at every point, soak the project

in prayer, listen to the whisper of the Spirit, and step out in faith.

One point of contact they had at once. Some of the residents in this town of 400 houses and one large synagogue, had once been patients at the Mission Clinic, and had listened to the good news in the little services held for outpatients there. So they recognised and welcomed Hannah and her friend.

After their morning's sortee, they drove out of town, and parked in the hot dust alongside some thorn plants covered with white snails. There, the pair of them relaxed for a while, and ate their picnic, before committing the afternoon's visitation to God in prayer. Once back on the streets, they met a German who recognised Caroline at once. She had been one of the nurses on his ward when he was a patient in a German hospital several years previously! The two ladies were discovering that their prayers for guidance were being answered.

It is true that they were rejected in two of the houses they visited that afternoon, and merely tolerated at two more. But at the other two or three, where the residents had been impressed by the loving witness of Jewish believers, Hannah and Caroline were warmly welcomed.

They drove back home late that afternoon with a sense of incredible relief and joy. One week later, she and a colleague drove up to the heights above Haifa to visit the bungalows of an older colony, perched among trees on a spur of Carmel, with wonderful views of the surrounding countryside.

The following day (October 22nd), they visited a much poorer settlement, situated on a low hill. Its wooden shacks had recently been attacked by Arabs. Many were derelict. The whole village seemed desolate. Her letter home showed that, once again, their presence elicited a warm response.

> At one little shop where I offered a tract called *The Way*, I asked the shop-lady if she knew the way to find the best possible thing in this world and the next. She laughed and said, 'You may tell me all about it, but I never like to keep any good

thing to myself. I must call these people outside.' I said she would make a good missionary! She called three young people standing near, and her husband, and although they were making fun of it, it was wonderful to get an audience, and I had a fine opportunity of witnessing.

When neither Sister Caroline, nor the Romanian sister, Ida Dreitschman, otherwise known as 'Sister Patience', were free to accompany her, Hannah was joined by a Jewish believer, Sister Peace. 'Frieda (Zeidan) was absolutely splendid,' Hannah wrote of her. 'She is young and attractive, and very much in earnest, and so brave.' Being fluent in both German and Hebrew, this shy and gentle Jewess proved a veritable diamond, reflecting in her whole personality the glory of the gospel she loved to share.

IV

Over the next two years, Hannah studied the maps, located the 173 Jewish colonies identified by the Jewish Agency, and set about visiting each in turn.

There were dangers. A missionary friend narrowly escaped death when snipers shot at her car up on Carmel. One bullet struck the iron wheel rim, another left a hole beside the clutch, while a third whistled through the open window above her head. Yet both driver and car escaped unhurt.

Likewise Hannah travelled many thousands of miles through inhospitable territory remote from any town and infested with political extremists, yet without being harmed in any way.

For all the distances she covered in her little car over eleven years, Hannah did not even have a burst tyre, though, on one memorable occasion, her little baby Austin stuck fast in the very marshlands by the river Kishon which had trapped Sisera's chariots in the days of Deborah. Hannah was distraught. She had not heard a shouted warning from a ploughman about the route she had decided to take. Nevertheless, the ploughman went to her aid. His two mules took fright at the bog and kicked out in all directions! A tractor from the neighbouring settlement also got stuck in the mire. Hannah's shoes were sucked off her feet. And, for all their shouting and heaving, the men could not budge the beleaguered baby Austin!

Hannah and Frieda resorted to some loud praying, and, to everyone's relief, the tractor wheels eventually gripped, and her precious little vehicle emerged in a woebegone state, thoroughly caked with cloying mud, but otherwise quite undamaged.

12   *Paper Time Bombs*

I

T he full story of Hannah's eleven year evangelistic enterprise is told in her graphic little book, *Wayfarer in the Land*. But nothing can compare with the letters she sent home on a regular basis, from which her father quoted so assiduously in the columns of the *Friends Witness*. They have all the vitality and immediacy of on-the-spot reporting.

Writing home in January 1938, for example, Hannah told of her excitement at receiving a letter from Ruth Laurence, a fellow graduate of Ridgelands Bible College, who also worked in Palestine. 'I nearly burst with praise when I read it two days ago,' she wrote. 'Isn't it just perfect how God works! He called me last April, and called L in May, and unbeknown to each other, gave us both the same charge!'

Only later, as they thought more about it, did the pair of them realise the snags involved. Both may have been called to the same kind of evangelistic outreach, but their personalities were never going to be a perfect match – unless it was the kind that sends everything up in flames! Ruth was the more senior, but Hannah the more experienced. And while Ruth was methodical, Hannah was anything but! Moreover, both liked to lead! Yet as they met to pray and plan, their partnership flourished, and once out on the job, their comradeship deepened. There is nothing like practical evangelism for fostering fellowship.

In the same letter home, Hannah also rejoiced in a very practical confirmation of their project.

> I have just had a lovely seal on the proposed Plain of Sharon campaign. The plan is for me to motor to Tel Aviv and back each week, staying there three days...But it is eighty miles each way, and I calculated that I would need £2, for petrol alone, for five weeks, on top of the other expenses of boarding in Tel Aviv and reaching the colonies. It seemed too expensive to manage...(Then) three days ago Mrs Rohold (who knew nothing about this) came to me and said, 'I have to give you £2 – sent anonymously from England for your work.' It was just like the Band days!

Then the letter went on to list the different districts in which the 173 settlements were situated. The number of districts underlined showed that in only fourteen or fifteen weeks, a start had been made on visiting six of the eleven areas, in itself an impressive achievement.

II

Hannah took special delight in visiting out-of-the-way settlements in remote districts where visitors were few and far between.

> On Monday, 21st February, we went to a Colony further away than any before...We knew one family and went first to their home. They had been patients of ours...We then visited from house to house during the limited time we had. We must have been to at least twelve houses, and in each people were kind and friendly, and took literature willingly. It was one of the happiest times of visiting we had. In these colonies, far off from the main roads, we were generally welcomed. They are so glad to see any strangers who take an interest in them.

As ever, Hannah had an eye for the beauties of nature all around them as they drove through the countryside that February.

It was perfect spring weather, and I cannot describe how beautiful the valley was, with green corn waving in the breeze and the Bedouin shepherds leading their flocks of sheep and goats through their green pastures. The recent rains had left lovely, clear, still streams and pools of water, and it was just like the 23rd Psalm turned into actuality! The banks were scarlet with anemones; and the hills, instead of showing bare and rocky, were green all over.

Like her Lord, Hannah also drew lessons for her work for God in Palestine from the work of God in creation.

Driving home through those miles of fresh corn, speaking of a coming abundant harvest, we were cheered to think that the seed of God's word will bring forth a great harvest too, and that we had been privileged to carry baskets of living seed to that colony.

But she was never allowed to become mawkishly sentimental about all the sheer loveliness of nature in which she constantly revelled, since there were constant reminders that 'nature is red in tooth and claw'.

One evening I drove out to a colony to fetch some people to a special meeting on Carmel. It was towards sunset, all the houses were gilded gold and the fields glowing. But the road was strewn with animal corpses. The jackals were running across the road, and further on a pack of wild dogs were tearing a dead donkey, and other poor creatures had been run over by motor cars.

In contrast, the sheep, though very vulnerable, were safe so long as their shepherd was with them.

I came to a bridge over the Kishon, and there the road was blocked by at least a hundred sheep. They were terrified by the car, but their shepherds led them to a green pasture at the side of the road, where they all waited in safety till I had passed by. And I thought it was as though the Lord said again: 'I am the Good Shepherd and take care of My sheep; you need fear nothing as you go to the colonies. I am with you to protect you.'

III

As the work progressed, Hannah was never short of volunteers. Workers from other missionary agencies were eager to get involved. The Society for the Free Distribution of Scriptures made her grants. Bishop MacInnes' daughter offered to help for a fortnight in early June.

Meanwhile, a Swiss worker accompanied Hannah in March, and managed to pacify one angry Polish Jewess who kept spitting and spluttering: 'May His name be blotted out,' every time Hannah spoke about Jesus. As a result, the Orthodox lady's two grown-up daughters apologised for their mother's behaviour, and requested Bibles for themselves!

A letter dated April 19th, 1938 spoke of another interesting encounter.

> God gave me a lovely little encouragement this morning. A few weeks back I was driving to Tel Aviv and gave a lift to a girl from a large Qibootz (sic) colony in that neighbourhood. I had an earnest talk with her, and she took two Bibles, one for herself and one for the Qibootz! She left (after taking my address in Haifa) saying 'I never expected such a treat when I set out this morning, and never dreamt that I should possess a Bible of my own!' Now this morning, there was a ring at the bell and there were two strange girls from that same Qibootz (fifty miles away). They said this girl had given them my address and had spoken of nothing else about her visit to a new colony, only this ride and contact and when she heard that her two friends were going to visit Haifa, she begged them to come and see me and bring her greetings and have a talk. I had a really wonderful talk with them. Both were about nineteen or twenty, and both were atheists, and yet of the wistful sort of atheist who wish they weren't.

Later on in April, Hannah was overjoyed to team up with her Finnish friend from Jerusalem again, Miss Ailie Havas. Because of illness, Ailie was due to return home later in the year, but begged to be involved in reaching the settlements around Galilee and down the Jordan valley before leaving the country. So they met up in Tiberias.

Sister Hope, as Hannah called her, was a perfect foil for her. As Hannah drove along the bumpy tracks listening for any suspicious engine noises, or the hiss of air escaping from a tyre, Ailie sat singing snatches of Christian songs, or commenting on the glory of the scenery! The fact that they happened to have wandered off the track in the process and ended up in Transjordan, was neither here nor there to Ailie! And, sure enough, the Police soon arranged their re-entry into Palestine! Then, when the Maskir of the Arab village they visited shortly afterward, roundly rebuked them for daring to venture into an area thick with dangerous animals, wild tribes, and trigger-happy gunmen, Sister Hope simply replied: 'But what does it matter if I lose my life as long as you have the opportunity to receive the word of God and hear about His gift of eternal life?'

At Beisan (Beth Shean) they roomed with two lady CMS workers, Hannah hogging the only bed, and Ailie stretching out on a thin mattress laid on the earth floor. Hannah never forgave herself for that, even though Ailie could not even remember the incident when Hannah subsequently apologised.

Meanwhile, they kept running out of Bibles. The Jewish settlers were eager to possess a copy of their own holy Scriptures. As one of them said, 'A Bible is not a book people can share, for we need to read it every day, and learn how in the holy land, we can live a holy life.'

At one colony, a resident bought a copy of the Old Testament (only) and insisted on taking Hannah's companion down to the orange grove, where he filled his arms with fruit. 'I mustn't wish you success in your work, because you are missionaries,' he said, 'but you have kindly let me have the Bible for half price and this is just a small return.' At another kibbutz, residents paid a shilling out of their annual fourteen shillings holiday allowance, to possess some portion of Scripture.

All this represented a change of attitude from previous years when kibbutzniks scorned the Scriptures. Now there was a new openness. 'The young people admire and even love Jesus, but utterly reject His deity,' Hannah wrote on April 29th, 1938. 'But as one said to Ailie, "We want to put His principles into practice, and we are more Christian than most Christians".'

In her last letter home before setting off for her annual leave in July that year, Hannah reflected on their record sales of Bibles in the colonies, and expressed her confidence in the power of God's word:

> Surely the time will come when the Holy Spirit will set those Bibles alight in the colonies. It is like laying up a store of dynamite of the power of God, which will one day explode and break down all opposition and hardness of heart.

13   *Across the Divide*

On her last night at home during the 1938 summer holiday, Hannah had attended the Railway Mission on North Hill in Colchester, and fastened on to Isaiah 55:12 as a word from God to her heart as she contemplated her return to the work of visiting Jewish colonies in Palestine: 'You shall go out with joy, and be led forth with peace' (KJV). It was to be a promise of particular relevance. War clouds were gathering. Dark forces were marauding. Palestine was seething.

The voyage back was eventful in itself. Mountainous seas in the early days forced Hannah to take refuge in her berth. Then when the storms subsided, the fogs descended. One night, their vessel narrowly avoided running down another ship. When she landed, it was clear that the country was in a state of deep unrest.

Ruth moved up from Jaffa so that she could go out to the settlements with Hannah. They found a suitable room for Ruth to rent in the home of a German doctor and his wife. Within a few days, their preparations were complete, so the pair of them went down to the bay for a dip, only to be stung by jellyfish!

Dr Churcher decided that in spite of the political unrest, it was probably safe enough for them to hit the road, certainly no more dangerous than living in Haifa itself. So for three or four days a week, Hannah and Ruth set out on the task of reaching the twenty or thirty colonies along the Megiddo Plain which they had planned to visit.

By December 28th, 1938, Hannah was able to report that over the previous fifteen months, she and sundry other workers had been able to visit eighty-five of the 143 Jewish settlements in the land without let or hindrance. Indeed, because men were not allowed to drive, Hannah's baby Austin car was often the only non-military vehicle to be seen on the roads. Policemen used to give friendly nods of recognition as her familiar car trundled by!

II

But the days they spent back in Haifa itself each week, were fraught. The clinic stood close to both the Jewish and Arab sectors of the city, so bomb outrages were not uncommon. Moreover, because the Arabs threatened to kill any Jews who visited the clinic or attended the meetings, Dr Churcher and his staff had to seek alternative accommodation.

In addition to dispensing food and clothing to hundreds of poor Jewish and Arab families in the city, Mrs Rohold also played her part by holding meetings for Arab women, praying that the meetings would encourage them to seek the ways of peace.

It is not difficult to understand the reasons behind this new upsurge of violence in the land. So far as Jewish people were concerned, events in Germany were reaching a crescendo. On Kristallnacht, November 9th, respectable Germans cheered when Jews were beaten up and their shops looted. Yet the British authorities in Palestine refused to admit more refugees from Germany. Indeed, the quota for Jewish immigration, fixed at 75,000 over five years, was suspended altogether for several months because so many refugees had entered the country illegally in order to escape from Nazi Germany. Plans to open camps for them in Africa were never realistic.

In 1937, the British Government had decided to partition

Palestine. But a year later, it bowed to Arab pressure, and changed its plan, to the disgust of Winston Churchill who accused it of 'breaking faith'. In such circumstances, its new plan to hold on to the Mandate, and to form a unified Arab-Jewish State in 1939, stood no possible chance of success.

As for the many peace-loving Arabs, they were often forced by their own terrorists to take part in acts of sabotage and violence, and then, when caught, were promptly punished by Britain's Palestinian police. It was all a no-win situation.

III

Clearly, the constant ill-treatment meted out to Jewish people by so-called Christian nations in both Europe and Palestine, proved a major obstacle to Hannah and her companions in their outreach. Yet, at the same time, the very upheavals and uncertainties experienced by everybody during the riots, somehow made people more receptive to the loving and confident witness of these two workers. As Hannah wrote in March 1939, 'We frequently find that when we visit a colony after it has been attacked, the people are solemnised and perhaps readier to listen.'

At Ramat David, one trenchant critic eventually relented and said how much he admired their faith. He had lost his own. 'It is strange to ask you who are Christians to comfort me,' he had said. 'But I have sought God, and cannot find Him.'

At another kibbutz, Ruth Laurence said she was beginning to discover what it means to be 'reviled' for the sake of Christ! But at Balfouria, near Afuleh, there was such openness to them that they were able to speak plainly about Israel's sin in rejecting Christ. In Sarid, their literature was gladly accepted, and conversations continued unabated. Even 'three grim bearded old orthodox Jews' in another village, listened to what they had to say, and accepted some booklets. A school teacher begged for two New Testaments so that she and a colleague could read parts about Jesus to their children. The daughter of a German Jewish believer wept as she spoke of her longing to be certain about Jesus.

In her annual newsletter, sent out on December 28th, 1938, Hannah summed up the spiritual mood they encountered at that time.

> It does seem that a remarkable movement is taking place in Israel – a movement of the Spirit of God, often quite apart from the work of missionaries. For instance, a well-known Jewish Doctor of Psychology in Haifa told Mr Plotke that she was struck by the number of Jewish patients who came to her in distress saying that they constantly dreamt of Jesus – and could she tell them what it meant? And last week, the leading Hebrew newspaper here published an article signed by the Jewish leaders of education in Palestine, urging all Jews to return to an earnest study of the Bible. They wrote that for 2,000 years Israel had neglected the Bible, and her spiritual life had become almost extinguished, and that her only hope is a return to the Word of God, and to teach it to her children. They urged that a chapter should be read and earnestly studied morning and evening, and stated that when Israel returns to the Bible, her salvation will be near. Since then, several orthodox Jews have written to the paper in shocked protest, maintaining that no one must read the holy book who is clean shaven, or without a hat, and many other rabbinical rules. But the fact remains that the leaders have made a public appeal to all Israel to study the Bible for themselves.

Just occasionally, Hannah and her helpers stumbled on information which showed that their work was bearing fruit. *Wayfarer in the Land* tells of one Jewish lady who was annoyed to discover that her visitors were missionaries. At the same time she felt sorry for them because they looked so hot and tired, and when they asked her for a drink of water, she was happy to oblige. But she seemed quite uninterested in anything the two of them had to say. However, they gave her a copy of the New Testament, and after they had left, she idly flicked over the pages, only to find herself reading the words of Jesus in Matthew 10:42. 'And if anyone gives even a cup of cold water to one of these little ones because he is my disciple, I tell you the truth, he will certainly not lose his reward.' She was quite taken aback, and decided to read the whole New Testament through from beginning to end, with the result that she came to faith for herself, and gathered neighbours together each week to study the Scripture with her.

IV

So, week by week, Hannah and Ruth went out with joy, and were led forth with peace. Near Zikron Jacob in March 1939, a fanatical Jew snatched a copy of the Scriptures and hurled it to the ground, saying the most blasphemous things about Christ. But the onlookers were so upset, they protested against him, and requested literature for themselves. At the children's colony nearby, twelve teachers begged for New Testaments, and listened to what Sister Faith, Ruth Laurence, had to say.

Remembering the anger one Jewish lady had shown a year before, Hannah took a bunch of roses to her house, and said 'I know you weren't very pleased to see me last time, but I've thought and prayed about you a lot, and would like you to accept these flowers.' To her delight, Hannah was invited into the house, where the lady concerned was pleased to accept a gospel and a booklet. In fact, while she still rejected those Jewish people who became 'Christians', her attitude towards Hannah was very friendly.

One man said to Ruth, 'Your work is not very easy, is it?' 'No,' she replied, 'but we love it, and it gives us great joy.' 'I can see that,' he said, 'but don't you mind being insulted?' 'Why should we?' she answered. 'As you know, our Lord and Master was insulted too.'

Hannah found great inspiration from the story of Joseph in Genesis. For the time being, Jesus, like Joseph, has hidden His face from His Jewish brothers. But there is a wonderful love in His heart for them, and one day, to their overwhelming relief and joy, He will make Himself known to His estranged brothers.

Normally, Hannah's Quaker principles prevented her from accepting any military protection as she drove around. But at the Syrian border, she had no option. The British insisted that she should toe the line! So she and Ruth drove round the precipitous hairpin bends up a steep mountain track in an army lorry, in order to make a whistle-stop visit to one very remote settlement. Once back in the valley after a hair-raising helter-skelter drive down, they realised it was impossible to get back to Haifa before curfew, so they put up in a small hotel.

Next day they visited a colony composed of rich Jews, who were reputed to be very anti-Christian. But they knew and respected Herr Löwenstein, President of the Hebrew Christian Alliance in Palestine, and that ensured a sympathetic audience for Hannah and Ruth. 'It made me realise the influence one earnest Christian life has on others,' Hannah wrote. 'We had a most happy time there, and we do praise God that He has enabled us to visit all the northern colonies.'

V

Little did Hannah realise then, that within a few weeks, the whole direction of her ministry was to shift dramatically yet again. In late Spring 1939, she fell ill, and had to spend several weeks in Nazareth Hospital. While there, she reflected on her task. The colonies in the north had all been reached, some more than once, and Sister Faith was due to travel south in order to visit the remaining settlements there.

Where should Hannah go from here? Ailie Havas had introduced her to work among Arab people in the Jordan valley, and Hannah had quite fallen in love with the romantic little town of Beisan, with its soaring hills, darting kingfishers and graceful gazelles.

As she mused, the fire burned. Clearly the gospel is 'to the Jew *first*.' But it is also to the non-Jew. And now that their work among all the Jewish settlements was nearing fulfilment, she became certain that the many hundreds of Arab villages throughout the land should also be reached.

It was, of course, a hopelessly impractical idea. To start with, she was unwell (some would say delirious!). Then too, the sheer number of villages envisaged, boggled the mind. Moreover, she scarcely knew a word of Arabic, and was woefully ignorant of Islam.

Yet when she broached the matter to Dr Churcher, he was, as ever, the great encourager. He even introduced her to the silver-haired Miss Bear, who had recently moved to Haifa with her Bible Woman, after spending many years working in Arab villages.

So in early May, the three of them set out for the village of Sileh, and a totally new style of ministry.

14 Highways and Byways

Hannah had secretly hoped that Dr Churcher would persuade her to postpone the start of her visits to Arab villages until after her summer holiday in England! But so far as he was concerned, the King's business requires haste. So he waved aside all her 'yes, buts', and insisted they made a start, even though Hannah was still weak after her recent hospitalisation.

They arrived at Sileh to find that the Head Man (Muktar) was in prison at Acre, and that two houses, where seventy-five rifles had been secreted, had been blown up by the security forces. In point of fact, Hannah and Miss Bear were the very first people to visit the village after the military raid. The Muktar's brother welcomed them warmly.

Hannah looked with horror at the fierce-looking men, all armed with daggers. Some wiry little boys presided over a pile of stones, and were preparing to pelt any unwelcome visitors. But in no time at all, the beaming Miss Bear was wowing them all with her giant-size 'Wordless Book'!

Her fluent Arabic was all gibberish to Hannah, of course, and squatting on the floor of a dark smoke-grimed upper room, without showing her legs and feet, proved incredibly difficult for her. In fact, 'Sister Piety' had to apologise for Hannah's protruding (though covered) feet! But Hannah had success with the children when showing them the little Bible picture books sent out to her by Sunday School children in England.

After an absence of ten years, Miss Bear was delighted to be back in the village of 2,000 people. The sound of coffee beans being pounded by a pestle in a mortar, had alerted the whole village to the fact that they had visitors! So everyone had congregated and begun sipping coffee from the same constantly-replenished little cup!

For Hannah, the whole experience was like an apprenticeship. She had led the way in visiting the Jewish colonies. But now she was reduced to the status of a chauffeur and onlooker, doing her best to soak up any Arabic words she happened to recognise!

Moreover, the contrast between the self-confident University-trained young people she met in many kibbutzim, and these childlike Muslim villagers, could not have been greater. The womenfolk they met in these dusty mud-brick houses, showed little awareness of spiritual realities, and could not concentrate for any length of time. They were just curious about Hannah and Miss Piety, fondling their hair and investigating their clothing. Hannah was experiencing culture shock once more.

Not that the Jewish settlements were entirely neglected at this time. Two or three days after this visit to Sileh, Hannah drove Miss Bear down to three new colonies in the Hedera district, the last one being the one hundredth Jewish settlement Hannah had visited.

By mid-June, still weak from her illness and constant travel, as well as the challenge of launching out on a new kind of work, Hannah was back in England for an extended holiday.

II

The outbreak of war in early September, created all kinds of problems for Hannah as she planned her return to Palestine. But eventually, after much form-filling, patient waiting and urgent praying, she had been able to catch the train from London on Wednesday, 4th October. In the course of the journey she led a lonely young soldier to the Lord.

At the docks there was a slight kerfuffle when the porter loaded Hannah's cases on to the wrong boat. Fortunately, the mistake was detected in time, and her luggage rescued. However, the ship was six hours late arriving in France, so she would certainly have missed her connection in France for Venice. 'But four of us were able to join in a taxi to Paris which only cost us 22/- each' (£1.10), she wrote. 'It was a glorious drive and we picnicked and God wonderfully opened the way to witness to them all. They were without faith and worried and anxious and very afraid. We reached Paris with four hours to spare.'

So, on Saturday, October 7th, Hannah and two Jewish people she had befriended on the cross-channel ferry, embarked at Venice for Haifa arriving there the following Thursday, October 12th.

Paradoxically, the start of war in Europe led to a lull in hostilities in Palestine. As David ben Gurion put it, 'we fought the war (alongside the British) as though there were no White Paper (about Palestine), and fought the White Paper as though there was no war.' But at least it was a war of words and not weapons at that stage.

Hannah's visiting schedule each week was prodigious. Within two weeks of landing, she and her companions had visited nine new colonies, two bedouin camps and one large Muslim town, as well as several villages.

On Mondays she was accompanied by Mrs Dorothy Pearson, daughter of Rev Samuel Schor, who had founded CMJ's 'Palestine Exhibitions'. Dorothy was the wife of Rev Leonard Pearson, who pioneered the Pentecostal Jewish Mission, now 'Focus on Israel', as well as 'The Bible through an Eastern Window' travelling exhibition. At the time, Leonard was serving as a policeman in Palestine.

On Tuesdays, Miss Bear and her Arab Bible Woman, 'Miss Mother of Hope', would go to an Arab village or bedouin camp with Hannah, often traversing dangerous terrain along rock-strewn tracks. 'It was wonderfully worth while to watch these simple ignorant people hearing the good news for the first time in their lives,' she wrote, 'and to hear an old man saying "Tell me that again and again, I must learn it," and then repeating, "The blood of Jesus Christ cleanseth me from all sin".'

Then on Thursdays and Fridays, Hannah visited Jewish settlements between Haifa and Tel Aviv in company with Miss Kate Graver of the American Baptist Mission, staying overnight at a central colony on the Plain of Sharon.

The fact that a second car was loaned to them, and that her father Samuel then sent a third car for their use, meant that three separate pairs of workers could now go out into the highways and byways of the Promised Land.

For Sister Piety (Miss Bear), the whole adventure was like a dream come true. She was able to travel by car with Hannah to the most inaccessible places, and to meet once more, men and women she had known many years before. 'Just the other side of Megiddo we found a new road leading into the heart of the mountains, with a signpost UM AL FAHM', Hannah wrote on November 5th, 1939. 'This was the first Muslim town Miss Bear had visited in Palestine thirty years ago. The road opens up a new district with twenty or more villages. We found people who remembered the visit of thirty years ago, and were taken to the house where Miss Bear had stayed. Imagine her joy!'

III

Hannah never lost her impish sense of humour. And she could take a joke against herself. They sometimes prayed that a man would be called to help them in their visiting, since car engines were 'an awful and alarming mystery' to her, and presumably a fellow could help when mechanical problems arose. But the one time a man went out with them, they promptly broke down!

They soon discovered that God could be trusted when testings came. On one occasion, they were able to replace a broken spring at Safed (Tsefat) only because a passing lorry driver had sold the proprietor a job lot of spares that very morning, including a spring which perfectly fitted Hannah's baby Austin!

At one remote Arab village, a toothless old lady looked Hannah up and down in a thoroughly critical manner, and then said to the Bible Woman: 'Is that your daughter you have brought with you from town? I suppose you are looking for a husband for her? But she is a bit old and ugly even for a village man.'

But Hannah was rather less amused when her missionary colleagues persisted in describing her adventures as 'Holy Picnics', until one of the Bible Women reminded her that, in spite of all the privations and dangers, when they could so easily be shot by a sniper or blown up by a land mine, the blessings poured out on them as they witnessed to Jesus, revelled in nature and celebrated good times, truly made their trips into veritable spiritual 'picnics'.

IV

Wayfarer in the Land gives little idea of the breadth and scope of Hannah's outreach, nor of the number of workers eventually involved in this work. At Tiberias Miss Lelly Wreshner, a Jewish believer who served with the Scottish Mission there, was enlisted. She and the American Kate Graver regularly visited settlements in the north. In Jerusalem (February 1940) twelve workers pledged themselves to pray for revival and to visit the villages: ten of them going to the Arabs and two to the Jews. At Jaffa, Dr and Mrs Wright set up a prayer group for this village ministry. Meanwhile, in four months, Ruth and Hannah themselves had visited seventy-one colonies and twenty-two Muslim villages.

On April 8th, 1940, she recorded in her diary that it had been exactly three years since God first called her to this work. How much had happened in that time! Six days later, she visited Ramallah with her good friend Miss Elizabeth Neatby. Then in early October, Ruth Laurence and Ailie Havas recommenced work north of Tel Aviv. So it went on.

In 1940, the quite large Arab congregation in Acre (Akko), which had experienced revival, pledged themselves to help Hannah in her work. Nine workers, including two women from the Brethren cause, evangelised villages round Nablus in May 1941. Eventually they reached seventy-two villages. Hannah's description is characteristically vivid:

> I have often wished I could paint or photograph the scenes in the villages when we sit down, and for the first time, they hear the gospel in their own village. Try and picture a large, dark, cool room, with a cement floor, glassless windows, a hole in the floor covered with ashes and cinders, on which the coffee jars stand, and fifty intent faces peering out of the semi-darkness, as all the chief men of the village and others listen to the message. We are all seated on the floor, some on mattresses, some on straw mats. Or again, a vine-covered open space in the middle of the village. There are again fifty or sixty men lying in the shade, listening quietly to the gospel message with very little argument. Always it is an unspeakable joy to watch them listening and to hear questions asked at the end, which prove they have at least understood something of the message.

V

In the course of all this vital activity throughout the war years, Hannah conceived a concern to open a Training Centre where unpaid workers could be trained in personal evangelism. Her words have since proved to be prophetic.

> It seems to me that if the Near East is really to be evangelised from end to end, it must be done by consecrated native Christians and not by a huge army of paid workers...It looks as though Foreign Missions may have to alter drastically in the future, and that there may not be vast sums of money to be used for salaried workers and large institutions...My hope is to open a little home where girls from different districts will

come for real Bible training, and teaching in Christian Service methods: then go home to their own towns and villages, and start little Sunday Schools and Cottage Meetings, etc., and even go out to surrounding villages.

She started to look for a suitable property. But the house near Nablus she wanted to rent, was eventually not leased to her. Meanwhile she travelled to Syria, sharing her vision, and subsequently heard that one Mission there had set aside two workers for village evangelism. Then she went to language school in Jerusalem in order to improve her Arabic.

She wondered about staying in the school for another term. But the call to go out into the villages was too strong to resist. So with Vera Schwarzstrauber, an American worker, she went up to Michmash, where the sullen faces of the men were softened by Vera's powerful preaching. 'It sometimes overwhelms me thinking what a privilege it is to be the first person to tell the amazing story of God's love and salvation to those who have never heard it before,' she wrote.

She knew protection on her little car as they journeyed. A one gallon can of oil which she bought, because no smaller one was available, proved invaluable when a heavy jolt cracked her oil tank. After sealing the leak as best she could, and constantly replenishing the oil, she was able to limp into a garage for repairs. Then when a vandal shattered the back window of her car, a British soldier replaced it free of charge. One day, someone noticed that one of the wheels was wobbly, so she removed the hub-cap and discovered that the wheel was hanging on by a single nut!

Meanwhile, her vision of a training centre persisted. An issue of the *Friends Witness* late in 1943, showed how the need was met.

> At the beginning of the year, it was No House; No Helper; No Students. Now the house is ready, and I hope Helen and two or three others, will be free to train in the New Year. We contemplate a three months' course, as so few young women can get away longer than that. In between times, refresher courses for Bible Women and Evangelists.

Soon Hannah's next venture was under way:

> Tomorrow (September 14th, 1943) I have to lay up the car, as none will be allowed without a permit. So ends five years of God's constant care and faithfulness, during which 975 places have been reached. I went to Rafidya to camp for two weeks with Helen Dadooche and Ellen Nassar. On the first day at Rafidya, God gave me a perfectly lovely little house, one of the prettiest I have seen in Palestine...It is surrounded by a lovely garden, and has a large cistern of water and perfectly lovely open mountain country all round. I am taking it for a year, believing it is God's will...I am so happy. As we finished the visiting to every place, and not till then, the house was given. I am hoping that a very nice Arab Christian woman in the village will come and work for me and shop in the Arab market. Rafidya is on 'bus routes, and some seventy villages can be reached.

When Ruth and Hannah met for their last morning of prayer together before launching this new work, their hearts surged with praise as they reflected on promises fulfilled and blessings bestowed.

15   A Blue Morris Van

Once the training home centred in the Arab village of Rafidya had run its course, Hannah moved on to her beloved Beisan.

In spite of some relaxation of the rules governing transport after the war, shortages continued to hamper village work. The cars were in constant need of repairs, but spares were hard to come by, except in the very flourishing and expensive black market. So two of the vehicles were sold off and the third kept going on petrol and prayer.

Hannah's colleagues got used to her 'dismal exhortations' about how they should ride in her precious car. But when the back axle finally broke, they decided it was time to pray for a replacement vehicle! So, on the strength of their conviction, Hannah went to the Morris agent in Jerusalem to negotiate. No, a saloon car was out of the question for at least two years. But she was offered £200 for her ageing heap if she would invest in this blue commercial Morris 8 van without side windows.

It was a little like asking a Duchess to ride in a sidecar. How unseemly for an aristocrat's daughter to be seen pottering around Jerusalem in a delivery van! But at least it was cheaper than a car. There was also plenty of room in the back to transport teams to the villages. It was even long enough for her to sleep in, if need be. So when her father and brother decided to chip in on the deal, she went ahead and bought the van for £460. She was not to know that its windowless sides would save human lives in future days.

At the end of December 1946, she held a special service at Christ Church, Jerusalem, to dedicate the vehicle. Then, ironically, just one month later, all British women and children were given four days to get out of the country! Jewish terrorists were now kidnapping British citizens and holding them hostage, in an attempt to end the Mandate. So her precious new van had to be mothballed for an indefinite period, while she and all others at risk, were flown to Egypt.

'Operation Polly', as it was called, inevitably became known as Operation Folly. Certainly the uncomfortable British military plane of doubtful vintage which transported the refugees, sorely tested Hannah's faith! But at least the evacuation gave Hannah the chance of a month's sightseeing in Egypt. Better still, it enabled her to go home to Hill House in March 1947 after an absence of eight years. Once there, she was able to be with her brother Bracy and his family for a while, before they emigrated to New Zealand later in 1947.

But Hannah had left her heart in the Holy Land. The time dragged by and often the news was dire. On March 2nd, martial law was imposed in some areas of the country. On April 24, the British barracks in Tel Aviv were blown up. On May 4, Zionist freedom fighters blasted their way into Acre prison and liberated 251 of their compatriots. An early return for Hannah looked unlikely.

When Elizabeth Neatby and Ruth Laurence joined Hannah at Hill House, they gave themselves to prayer for events in the land of their adoption. And when CMJ let it be known that they were looking for a housekeeper at their hospital in Jerusalem, to replace one who had been there almost thirty years, Hannah took the need on board, never suspecting that while her application to go back as an evangelist would be turned down, an urgent plea for her to become that very hospital housekeeper, would set her dove-cotes fluttering!

The idea was preposterous, of course. She could boil a kettle, and even manage to run a small Arab mud hut for two.

She had done so at Beisan. But any more complicated domesticity was beyond her. As for a hospital, that was something for experienced professionals, not for incompetent amateurs like herself!

She laughed out loud when the letter arrived asking her to go as housekeeper, and her father was most upset by her levity. But he also realised that the idea was out of the question. He preferred her original option of going to Syria as a village evangelist, and waiting for the chance to slip back into Palestine as soon as events made it possible. Her gift was to be an evangelist, not a housekeeper!

But on reflection, Hannah concluded that life in a mission hospital presented many opportunities for Christian witness. Moreover she knew the main languages required for this role (Hebrew, Arabic, German and English). And she was assured that the former housekeeper had trained her staff superbly. In the end, Hannah offered her services on the understanding that all concerned clearly recognised that she was manifestly unqualified and unsuitable for the role.

So, after seven months away from the land of her love, she found herself driving up the mountain road to Jerusalem, with a heart singing its praise to 'Him who alone doeth great wonders' (Psalm 136:4, KJV).

II

For six weeks, the departing housekeeper inducted Hannah into her new role. Then, on the day she handed over the keys and left, November 29th, 1947, the Partition of Palestine was announced, and everything changed.

Hannah was woken up at 1.30 next morning, Advent Sunday, by the sound of unrestrained revelry. Horns were blaring. Crowds were chanting 'Long live Israel'. People were riding on the roofs and bonnets of cars as they inched along the crowded streets. The hospital compound was like ancient Jericho, 'straitly shut up. None went out, and none came in.'

Sleep was impossible, of course. But when it was time for

morning service, nothing would stop Hannah from attending Christ Church in the Old City. She elbowed her way through the milling throngs, and eventually reached the quiet oasis just inside Jaffa Gate, opposite the Citadel.

It was another world. The worship caressed her spirit. Blind girls from Beit Jala sang 'with lovely, touching voices: "Jesus is coming again".' Hannah found herself longing that soon the crowds in Jerusalem would be welcoming their Messiah with equal abandon to that shown in the west of the city that morning.

Next day, the Arab counter-demonstrations began, and seven Jews were killed. The die was cast. Now that the British had announced the end of the Mandate in six months' time, Jews and Arabs were girding themselves for war. Crowded mosques were harangued with inflammatory speeches. Acts of terror were perpetrated by both sides. Barriers went up between the two communities.

Because Assad could no longer amble down to the Arab market with the hospital donkey each day, Hannah did the shopping in her blue Morris van with the frightened Assad crouching in the back, minus his Arab headdress and dreading discovery.

Clearly the hospital's Arab staff needed to be evacuated. So, by the end of December, Hannah had smuggled them back to their home villages, hidden in her blue van with its windowless sides! Meanwhile, the CMJ Girls School moved up from Christ Church on December 8th, and occupied two empty wards in the hospital.

Hannah was kept busy running a taxi service for missionaries and friends with their belongings; and when a curly little black and white mongrel, left behind by an evacuee, made its home with Hannah, he too accompanied her sundry expeditions.

Hannah remarked that, like a lot of animals, Charlie possessed an uncanny ability to suss people out straight away.

With the Hagana (Jewish defence forces) he was polite but slightly aloof. At the British barricades all the guards naturally spoke to Charles before bothering about me, and he allowed himself to be petted and stroked in a condescending fashion. At the sight of an Arab guard in a red headdress with a gun in his hand, advancing towards the van, Charles would withdraw his head, and when the man stooped down and put his face to the window to look inside, he would leap forward in a frenzy of indignation, with a bark far too large for his small body. If it were a new guard, the man, at this sudden onslaught, would leap back as though he had been shot, amid delighted roars of laughter from his companions (*Watchman on the Walls*, p 25).

In January 1948, the hospital closed, and because their own Hadassah Hospital on Mount Scopus was now behind Arab lines and inaccessible, the Jewish Authorities took over CMJ's hospital on The Street of the Prophets.

Conflict raged in the city. Casualties mounted. Ambulance sirens wailed night and day. Car bombs exploded in nearby streets. Danger stalked their every move.

Hannah was glad to have a free weekend when she could meet up with Ruth Laurence, now back in the land and living at Tel Aviv. On the way she was shot at, searched and arrested. But nothing could dim her joy when the two ladies eventually greeted each other at Immanuel House, and then spent a day wandering among the flowers on the Plain of Sharon.

But a subsequent journey to Gaza to take a ward maid back to her home, was even more fraught. The road was under constant sniper fire. Guards constantly checked her cargo and documents. Coming back, a field of corn suddenly erupted as armed insurgents, previously hidden from view, sprang to their feet and advanced towards her little van while she waited to fill up with petrol. But although the convoy ahead was attacked, Hannah herself escaped.

Not all Christian workers were similarly spared, however. One of the teachers at the Girls School was shot on her way to morning worship at St George's Cathedral. Next day, a prominent mourner at her funeral, was also shot dead.

Hannah decided to get away to Nablus to pray for 'a hearing heart', and to ponder her stance in this relentless conflict. Should she continue to live on the Christ Church compound behind Arab lines? Or should she move back to the hospital inside the Jewish city?

III

Once more, Hannah braved the sniper fire, and made for the Shechem Road. As she headed north, past the settlements where bullets had narrowly missed her van on a previous journey, Hannah rested on the Bible passage in Ezra 8:22,31 which she had read that morning. She felt no need of military protection so long as the hand of God was upon her for good. And so it proved, for she was delivered from the hand of the enemy 'and of such as lay in wait by the way' (KJV).

It was good to spend time in quiet reflection once more, as she wandered through the olive grove with its carpet of tiny but brilliant flowers. She was not far from the village of Rafidya, where she had lived four years previously. The lovely scenery, so familiar to her from years gone by, brought refreshment to her spirit.

Gradually she became sure that her place was to be beside the Jewish people in their hour of need. She had no great expectation of success, so far as their attempt to build a State was concerned. Like most non-Jews, she believed that the Arabs would almost certainly overwhelm them. But she believed it was her Christian responsibility to pray for them to come together as a people. Above all, she wanted the breath of God to come on the people of Israel so that they might experience a spiritual renewal (Ezek 37).

So she made up her mind to live in West Jerusalem once more, in spite of the dangers involved. When she arrived back in the city, she found that plans were afoot to evacuate all Hebrew Christians (Messianic Jews). And by the beginning of May, fighting was so intense, Hannah could delay her departure from Christ Church no longer.

Taking two black hens, Jemima and Keren-Happuch, four pigeons, and a yellow and white kitten called 'Mercy', as well as her ever faithful Charlie, Hannah drove her blue van out of the Arab Old City into the Jewish West Jerusalem, where she joined Ruth Clark, the headmistress, and Rev Ronald Adeney, the CMJ Minister, who were already living in a doctor's house on the hospital compound.

The hens duly laid eggs (most days), the kitten kept mice and rats at bay, and the pigeons' broods supplemented their meagre rations. As for Charlie, when shells and bullets ravaged both the wards and the dwellings of the hospital, his presence in Hannah's warm embrace, brought comfort to them both!

With the end of the Mandate on May 14th, and the proclamation of the new State of Israel by David ben Gurion the following day, hordes of Arab forces from neighbouring countries poured into the land, and threatened to devour the old-new nation at birth.

For a month, Jerusalem was totally besieged. The main road from Tel Aviv was blocked. Supplies were cut off, and the water pump at Latrun was blown up. Stark disaster stared Israel in the face.

Yet for all the nightly terror that descended, even on a hospital, Hannah knew an inner calm.

> I used to try and imagine what things would be like when the British left and real war began. Well it is all happening as I imagined, but what I didn't foresee, though I ought to have done so, was all the joy and peace the Lord gives, and the continual sense of His presence and help. Nor did I foresee how much I would prefer to be in the Jewish side of the city, nor the pleasure I got in the cooking and housework. Everything that goes on is intensely interesting, and life is over-flowingly full. Our home is a little heavenly oasis in the midst of the Valley of the Shadow of Death. The streets are deadly dangerous places, the hospital just next door reeks of death, and the mountains round about Jerusalem are full of

armies and gun emplacements. But inside our green fences there is something I cannot describe, but which makes me worship and rejoice, and fills me with steady happiness. I think Dr Moffatt's translation of Philippians 3:20 best describes it: 'You are A COLONY OF HEAVEN' (*Watchman on the Walls*, p 76).

16   *End of An Era*

After eight months cooped up in Jerusalem, with bullets and shells constantly threatening life and limb, Hannah was glad to set out for a holiday in Haifa on October 28th, 1948.

She joined a group of friendly passengers travelling to Tel Aviv by taxi. On the way, they passed the village of Qastal, perched on an eminence about the highway. Arab gunmen had used it to ambush Jewish convoys grinding up hill towards the capital. Now it was in ruins.

Hannah recalled that Qastal had been one of the last villages she and her companion had reached with the gospel. They had sat in a smoke-blackened room, sharing the good news, while the womenfolk had prepared food for a wedding. They were not to know then, that some of their audience would soon be wielding guns, not Bibles.

The taxi turned left to avoid Arab insurgents holed up by the roadside at Latrun, and made for the 'Burma Road'. Throughout the siege, this new road, though constantly attacked by Arab militias, had been Jerusalem's lifeline.

At one point, their taxi pulled up behind a queue of cars, and Hannah was able to see that President Weizmann's limousine was just ahead of them. But while she caught several glimpses of the President's trilby, she didn't see his face.

Once at Tel Aviv she changed to a Sheroot taxi heading north along the coastal road. After an hour or so, the familiar

hills loomed into view, and the Plain of Sharon began to narrow. Soon she was climbing up to the Mission House at Haifa
where she had started her apprenticeship as a temporary
worker nearly seventeen years before!

For months Hannah had lived hand to mouth, with
scarcely time to breathe. Now she could greet old friends,
catch up on all the news, and stride out on to the hills, with
her Bible and notebooks, to spend quality time in prayer.

She sat in the shade of a tree, gazing out on the wide
sweep of the bay, and felt the tensions ease away from her.
Once again, the Bible leapt to life as she sought the Lord.
'Never in all my life have I had a holiday so radiantly and con-
tinuously illuminated by His presence,' she wrote. Moreover,
a new and deeper love for Israel and its people, took root in
her heart during those three weeks.

Hannah had been one of only twelve ex-patriate missionaries allowed to continue living in Jerusalem throughout the
War of Independence. Now, as she watched the boats bringing in yet more refugees, she realised that this Arab-Israeli
conflict constituted the birth pangs of a new era in the Holy
Land. Part of the strip of Palestine west of the Jordan, was
now 'Israel'. Talk of 'missionaries' was becoming wholly
inappropriate. The future lay with indigenous groups of local
believers worshipping in their own way, and reaching out to
their own peoples.

At the outset, Hannah had not believed that the Jewish
people would succeed in their bid to establish a state of their
own. But now their dream was a reality, and Hannah had to
revise her whole perception. From studying the prophecies,
she reached the conclusion that Israel's return in unbelief
was just as Ezekiel in particular had envisaged (36:22-24).
She also saw that beyond the miracle of their national
revival, there was to be the even greater miracle of Israel's
spiritual restoration (36:25-28). The dry bones of the nation
were certainly coming together with a most unholy cacoph-
ony! But now they needed the breath of God to come upon

them in such a way that they would come alive to God and act as His champions (37:1-14).

II

Hannah's first letter from home for many months, had arrived on July 20th, 1948. Within a week, regular postal services between Israel and Great Britain were established. Then in January 1949, just a few weeks after returning from her holiday in Haifa, Hannah received the letter she most dreaded. Her beloved father had died on Thursday, January 13th, in his seventy-ninth year.

It was too late for her to attend his funeral. Sea voyages were too slow, and regular air services to England were not yet in operation. But with considerable ingenuity, she planned her route home via Cyprus, Athens and Paris. In the event, their ageing plane could not land in Cyprus because of bad weather, and as there was too little fuel on board to reach Athens (due to the war, Israel was desperately short of oil), the plane was forced to land behind enemy lines at Beirut. Along with the rest of the passengers, Hannah was detained overnight, before being sent on to Greece without any food on board. Not until they reached France, could they transfer to what Hannah called a 'proper' aeroplane!

Once at home, Hannah spent two months helping to sort out her father's business affairs. But it was heavenly to be back at Hill House in an English spring-time.

Her father had decreed that the splendid old Georgian home which Hannah loved so well, should become a Christian guest house, which Marjorie would run. In particular, he had wanted the twenty room house to be a 'Rest Home' for Christian workers, where missionaries and ministers who were under stress, could seek refreshment of spirit. So this was to be the last time that Hannah could call Hill House her own 'home'. Yet again, she was coming to the end of an era.

She thought of the tree house in one of the tall chestnuts

in the garden where she and her sisters loved to play when they were young. Ever the little rebels, she and her younger sister, Naomi, had once denuded Samuel's prize azaleas of their blooms when he had asked them to tidy up the bushes in readiness for a missionary garden party. 'Why can't the three gardeners get rid of all the dead blooms?' they'd reasoned. So off came the living heads too!

How could she ever forget her dear fifty-five year old mother, propped up on pillows, looking out on to the island and pond by means of a mirror strategically placed by her bedroom window? Rose had so loved the colour-rich beauty of rhododendrons and lilies of the valley streaming into her room and lighting up her remaining weeks on earth.

Every nook and cranny of the grounds was special to Hannah herself. On each long furlough, she had spent her quiet times in the garden, communing with her Lord. Now she would have to share it with an endless succession of guests and visitors. 'So where will you live?' her older sister Ruth asked her one day. 'I suppose my roots are deeper in Israel now than anywhere else,' she replied, 'and as I have the right to live there now, I think I shall do so.' She wasn't to know that even this right would soon be denied her.

Meanwhile, she was none too sure that Marjorie would cope with all this new responsibility. She had kept house for the Rector of Lexden, then for her father and brother who worked on a farm. But not even her time spent in Bible College would have prepared her adequately for the business of running a guest house.

Much as she loved Marjorie, Hannah had never realised her very considerable qualities, as Samuel had done. He had quickly come to appreciate Marjorie's gracious, thorough, no-nonsense, and practical wisdom. She had taken over so many of the everyday details which some of Samuel's housekeepers had sadly neglected, and she had, in his own words, proved such a great comfort to him. Hence he relied on her judgment. Moreover, as Hannah was to discover, Marjorie herself knew divine resources which enabled her to cope with divine responsibilities.

In early May, Hannah set out for the airport to fly back to Israel, before the first guests began to arrive at Hill House, but not before Marjorie had locked up Hannah's room with all her personal possessions, so that she would always have a home of her own at Hill House, and had promised to continue Samuel's practice of writing to Hannah every week: a promise she faithfully kept for forty-one years.

III

As her plane touched down at Zurich airport en route to Israel, Hannah was delighted to see her friend Lilly waiting to greet her.

Ever since her childhood holidays in Switzerland, Hannah was always glad to be among the lakes and mountains she loved so well. Now she was to savour three wonderful weeks with her dear Swiss colleague, catching up on news, preparing for the hardship of a land still at war, breathing in the mountain air, and storing up precious imagery, later to find expression in her books: *Hinds' Feet on High Places* and *Mountains of Spices*.

But Lilly could not wait to fill Hannah in on her own agenda. A Christian teacher in Switzerland had begun teaching believers the necessity of thanking God in any and every situation, in bad times as well as good, for it is the rejoicing heart that is the receiving heart.

Hannah was none too impressed at first. How can anyone possibly bubble over with gratitude to God when the bottom has just dropped out of his or her world, or some major calamity has seemingly blighted the whole of life?

But the more she considered it, the more right it seemed to be. Did not the Psalmist bless the Lord at *all* times? And hadn't Paul taught believers to give thanks for *all* things? Any other attitude toward life's upheavals, looked suspiciously like a bad attack of self-pity. In any case, there is always *something* in life for which to thank God.

So she took the principle on board, without asking whether this particular remedy was the right prescription for her present malady. And in Hannah's case, the medicine was destined to produce an adverse reaction. By blithely ignoring underlying tensions and traumas in her present experience, Hannah was in danger of building up an inner ferment, which was bound to explode.

The fact was, that Hannah needed to come to terms with her grief. As the Preacher said, 'There is a time to weep, and a time to laugh; a time to mourn, and a time to dance' (Eccles 3:4).

With characteristic honesty, Hannah admitted that she found it very difficult to implement this new principle of thanking God for everything, once she got back to the hospital. What really upset her was that while all the other workers automatically assumed that they had the right to go back to their own ministries now that the Sincere Truce had started to normalise everything in Israel, they took it for granted that she would stay on as housekeeper.

Hannah felt they were being unreasonably thoughtless. And when one of them said, 'You know, Hannah, that in God's sight it is just as much "missionary" work to do the housekeeping and the shopping and stand for hours in queues, as it is to preach the gospel,' her volcano erupted!

'In which case, why don't you give up your particular job and do the housekeeping yourself?' the ungracious Sister Grace retorted!

It was all so unfair! Surely, nothing could be more important than her evangelistic outreach. So why should she be forced to give it up? In the end, she became so embittered that one of her colleagues told her quite plainly that she was becoming almost impossible to live with – a stinging rebuke which, however kindly administered, was scarcely calculated to ameliorate her feelings!

At the same time, Hannah knew that any failure to overcome this inner resentment was bound to affect all her relationships. If she was to have a spiritual ministry among her colleagues, then she would need 'a heart at leisure from itself to soothe and sympathise', and at this particular moment in time, that was just what she did not have.

'So there came the last desperate struggle with pride, resentment, bitterness and self-pity,' she wrote in her second autobiography. 'The five long years of strain through the mounting terrorism, the tension of the last months of the Mandate and the twelve months in besieged Jerusalem, my father's death, and the loss of my home in England, and now the loss of my special work in Israel, all culminating in this dreadful climax that I had become *impossible to live with*!'

It was not to be her 'last desperate struggle', of course. Human pride does not give up that easily, and there were plenty more battles to follow! But it marked a major step forward in her personal pilgrimage. She knew she had to grieve properly for those several areas in life where she was suffering deep loss. Then, having reached the point of 'acceptance', the final outcome of her situation could safely be entrusted to her heavenly Father, even if it meant staying on as an unpaid housekeeper for the rest of her time in Israel.

As it happened, the answer came more quickly than she could have expected. 'At last, by His grace, the bitter cup was drunk,' she wrote, 'and in less than three months another experienced worker was able to join the group and to undertake the housekeeping.'

So she took leave of Jerusalem, headed north in her blue van, settled in a lovely white cottage in Tiberias, planned her work of visitation to neighbouring settlements, and gave herself to the writing of her wonderfully moving life-story, *The Hearing Heart*.

17 Keswick 1951

After a few weeks' quiet rest overlooking the Sea of Galilee, Hannah returned to her attic room in Jerusalem, where, up on the flat roof and in the shade of a giant eucalyptus tree, she laboriously turned her handwritten story into a typewritten manuscript. As the slightest breeze rippled the silver-grey leaves of the tree, she prayed that her own life would also respond with heavenly sensitivity to the breath of the Holy Spirit whispering deep in her hearing heart.

That August, she spent in retreat high up on the slopes of Mount Olympus in Cyprus away from every kind of distraction. And it was there that she entered into a new and deeper experience of God.

When the War of Independence had ended, Hannah had joined workers from other societies in a series of evangelistic services and prayer meetings which sought to give expression to the oneness of all believers. But denominational differences and missionary rivalries sadly rendered this experiment largely ineffective.

So Hannah and her two colleagues in CMJ, began to pray more earnestly for a new and deeper experience of God's power in their lives. But contrasting views of what this might mean for them, also began to surface as they met together for prayer. One stressed the mighty works which result from the fullness of the Holy Spirit. Another believed that all barriers between God's people would be swept away once they were baptised in the Spirit. Meanwhile Hannah yearned for a richer experience of God's love in her life.

In the event, this is precisely what happened to her as she sought God's face on Mount Olympus. There came such an infusion of holy love, that every part of her glowed with a deep inner radiance. She felt herself reaching out to all the world with total acceptance. The description of Paul's Pentecost in Romans 5:5 summed up her new experience quite perfectly. She could now say with the apostle from the very depths of her being, that 'the love of God is shed abroad in our hearts by the Holy Spirit which is given unto us' (KJV).

The way she expressed this new outpouring in her life, was happily free from undue triumphalism at that time. She contented herself with saying that 'like Hannah of old, she cradled a small weak child of Love in her heart which she dedicated to the service of God.' She also realised that any experience that is genuine, must have genuine results in one's life. And gradually it occurred to her that, just as Hannah had given birth to other children beside Samuel, she too was to have other 'children' in the shape of those books she would be gifted to write.

As it happened, she was to write some twelve books in ten years. At first no publisher was willing to take them on. But her own Society, CMJ, brought out one of them, *Watchman on the Walls*, that same year (1950), which was her diary of the war years in Jerusalem. Her first autobiography, *The Hearing Heart*, was published just over two years later. As a result, hundreds of thousands of readers were wonderfully enriched, and the Society too was blessed.

II

Once back from Cyprus, Hannah settled in the little white cottage owned by the recently reopened Church of Scotland Hospital in Tiberias. From there she reached out to more than sixty villages, accompanied from time to time by willing volunteers from the hospital staff.

It was a time of new openness. The Jewish people were feeling less 'defensive' and more receptive now that they lived in a home of their own. Hannah also felt herself to be a new woman, imbued with a new love, especially for Jewish people.

Moreover, she was enjoying new explorations in her reading. Among the books she discovered on the hospital shelves, were some by A.J. Gossip and George MacDonald. Their emphasis on God's Fatherhood, and the Kingdom of Love, chimed in with her own new perspectives. Her sister Naomi, now living and teaching in Oxford, also sent copies of books by C.S. Lewis to Hannah as and when they came out, though to Hannah's regret, she sent none of the *Narnia Chronicles* or space age odysseys, which she therefore promptly purchased for herself!

Hannah's mind was opening up to new horizons of theological thought. She was particularly taken with Lewis's book, *The Great Divorce*, which she read three or four times straight off.

Then came her final visitation to an Orthodox Jewish community. It was the first time she had made such a venture entirely on her own, and she shrank from the apparent foolhardiness of going there. It is true that she had fully identified with the Jewish people throughout their recent struggles. But it seemed sheer presumption on her part to intrude on people who had been faithful to their own religion when persecuted so relentlessly by so-called Christian countries.

After parking alongside a mimosa bush, and committing herself in prayer to this difficult task, she drove up to the settlement, and with tears in her eyes, apologised for her rudeness in daring to offer copies of the Gospels to them when so many adherents of the Christian faith did not always follow the teaching of those very Gospels in their own lives.

'I do hope you will forgive me,' she said, 'but this means more to me that I can possibly say. I shall be so glad if you will take these books, and if you and the others will read them and see if it is not exactly what the world most needs.' To her joy, they willingly accepted not only the literature, but also her loving approach.

A fortnight later, two of her tyres burst, and as no replacements were to be found, the vehicle was out of commission. Then a doctor from the hospital told her that some new workers would be requiring the cottage she was renting. So Hannah had no option but to look for another home.

After a day spent in prayer, she decided to go back to England, realise some of the securities her father had left her, and buy both a car and a caravan. In that way she would have a roof over her head, and could travel around enlisting 'Intercessors for Israel'.

Yet again, the inner voice confirmed her settled choice, and that familiar sense of peace brought reassurance.

> From the balcony of the flat I looked out on another of the loveliest views in the country. Below me lay the shining blue waters of the Sea of Galilee, and beyond them to the north, rose the white peak of Mount Hermon, towering skywards, majestic and pure white, like 'a great throne, high and lifted up'. It was a cloudless, sunny winter day. The whole scene was breathtakingly beautiful, and as I walked excitedly up and down the balcony, my heart was exulting and mounting up on wings of joy and relief, and the seagulls sweeping over the lake on their flashing white wings seemed to mirror back to me the same joy.

III

Her six month stay in England brought Hannah enormous happiness, and not a few surprises. She discovered that having other people stay in Hill House actually enhanced her sense of 'home-coming' there. And as she watched Marjorie 'ministering so lovingly and happily to the guests, and finding such joy and satisfaction in the service', she realised that the decision to make her home into a Christian guest house, had been exactly right.

In addition, Hannah found that her little book which CMJ had published the previous year, *Watchman on the Walls*, was proving very popular, and because she was now on hand in England, she was able to take advantage of the many new doors for ministry which the book was opening up for her.

But because relationships between the British Government and Israel were not good, her plans to buy a car and a caravan, faced difficulty. To start with, there was a long waiting list for new cars in England, and Hannah's needs came low down on the scale of priorities. Moreover, because Israel had been put out of the sterling area, it was not possible for her to cash in her securities, so that, even if by any chance a car was available, she did not have the money to pay for it. A vehicle, donated to her by a missionary who'd been posted to another country, was claimed back by the garage because another client was next on their 'foreign quota list', and so had prior claim on it.

Later, a car and two caravans were given to her by prayer supporters at Keswick. But it proved difficult to get both export and import licences for them. Then her brother's illness forced Hannah to change all her plans in early 1952, and the money she had set aside to pay for the licences, had to be used for buying her air ticket to New Zealand. One of the caravans did eventually end up in Israel, where it was used by CMJ workers. But her own car and caravan never made it.

IV

Undoubtedly, the highlight of her stay in England, was a return visit to the Keswick Convention in July 1951. It was sheer heaven to stroll through the streets, greeting old friends, browsing at the many side stalls run by missionary societies and religious booksellers, drinking in the glories of Lakeland, which was looking at its best that year, and revelling in the worship and ministry.

Hannah was no longer terrified of the milling crowds. Little Miss Much-Afraid was proving more than conqueror through Him who loved her. Not even warfare, danger, and now, homelessness, could rob her of that inner joy which the Shepherd had given her. Now her lameness was healed, and she had hinds' feet. Her crooked mouth could communicate without any sign of contortion.

Twenty-seven years had gone by since the never-to-be-forgotten Convention of 1924, when she had knelt by her bed reading 1 Kings 18, and had resolved to follow the Lord. How strange that seven-and-a-half years later she had gone to live at Haifa, within easy reach of the very site where Elijah had challenged the prophets of Baal, as described in that chapter.

Did Hannah reflect on all that when Canon Guy King announced his text at the Thursday evening meeting: 'Then the fire of the Lord fell' (1 Kings 18:38, KJV)? With that easy, relaxed and gentle way of his, the much-loved little preacher pointed out that the fire fell when the altar was prepared, the sacrifice was offered – piece by piece, the water was poured on the altar so that only supernatural fire could consume the sacrifice, and when prayer was made. But even the prayer could not avail so long as there was still an 'I' left in it (as there was in verse 36). Only as Elijah's motive was cleansed, so that the glory should be God's alone (v 37), did the fire of heaven fall. Hannah's whole life-story was in fact a vivid commentary on the reality of that message.

Meanwhile a note had been passed to her at the supper table one evening. Would she be prepared to speak at the great missionary meeting on the Friday, in order to represent work among Jewish people? She felt overwhelmed at the privilege being given to her. Now she could repay a little of the debt she owed to Keswick, and could share something of what God was doing in the land where Jesus once lived.

Did it also occur to her that she had just spent time serving in the very hospital about which Dr Orr-Ewing had spoken in the Missionary Meeting that had changed her life twenty-seven years previously?

'The great day arrived. Each speaker was allowed only seven minutes, and I was warned that a red bulb would glow on the reading desk at the end of six minutes, and then I must bring my brief message to a fitting conclusion,' Hannah wrote. But those who knew her well, could have predicted what followed! The light shone brightly and persistently, but Hannah carried on like a ship in full sail!

It was after that meeting, and her seven (or was it eight, nine or even ten?) minute talk, that a lady promised Hannah the gift of a car for her work in Israel.

V

That particular convention was also of special significance to a troubled young man of eighteen who was grappling with an enormous spiritual crisis.

His father had died at the age of forty-two, when he himself was only twelve. His teenage years had been spent cooped up in a narrow environment, with a grieving mother, and an uninspiring lifestyle. Then, when driving a van one day, he had been involved in a serious accident, in which a young cyclist was badly injured. Scarcely a night went by without him reliving that appalling experience, waking up in terror, and calling out in anguish. It seemed that his mind would cave in under the burden of near despair.

However, some friends had driven him by car from his home in Essex to the Keswick Convention, 300 miles away, where, for the first time in his life he savoured the beauties of Lakeland. He couldn't get over the fact that there was a lovely mountain looming outside his bedroom window at the back of their guest house! He also discovered that there were many more Christians than the handful of earnest believers he knew in his own particular little chapels in Essex. And everybody in Keswick seemed to be walking around with a Bible under his arm, and a smile on his face! As for the worship, he had never sung so many beautiful hymns, or heard such heart-touching ministry.

Most mornings, they motored along gated roads, among soaring fells and by glistening lakes. Sometimes he rowed a boat on Derwentwater. Each day he drank in the atmosphere of the meetings.

Back home, he had been led to expect scintillating experiences the moment he got 'saved'. But while God was real, the Bible precious, and Christ the greatest reality of his life, he knew no soaring joy, no throbbing assurance, no mind-blowing ecstasy. But at Keswick, he gradually came to see that standing before God depends on faith, not feelings, and that faith takes God at His Word.

Perhaps it was those breezy afternoon studies in the life of Abraham which Dr Donald Grey Barnhouse of Philadelphia gave, mainly for the benefit of day visitors, which made the penny drop. Certainly he had never listened to such a dynamic expositor in his life. The American stood there, a cuddly bear of a man, with crinkly hair, rattling out his sentences as from a machine gun, his knees pumping up and down as though riding a mountain bike, a half smile always playing around his lips, and trenchant challenges constantly punctuating his messages. No one fell asleep when he took the platform, however hot and long the afternoon might be! And of course, the theme throughout was the Patriarch's trust in the Living God by which alone he was accounted 'righteous'.

All kinds of other influences were brought to bear on him that week: the tender pathos of George Duncan's Christ-like ministry, Fred Mitchell's Bible reading on the Revelation which he heard on the Thursday morning (making him regret that he missed the previous three expositions in that series), and the cockney preacher Stanley Baker of 'The Essex Five' who spoke at the open air meeting one evening.

At one of the side-stalls he acquired a copy of *The Life of Faith* weekly paper which he devoured from cover to cover. Later he took it regularly, explored the Scriptures through its 'Life of Faith Bible School', and eventually became quite a regular contributor to the paper himself.

Above all, he bathed in the wonderful sense of 'togetherness' that prevailed in the meetings. And the deep sense of 'belonging' which he had needed so much, helped to bring healing to his heart.

The Missionary Meeting on Friday morning was something else! He had never met a missionary in his life. Now he heard a dozen of them, and saw dozens more! Fred Mitchell, the Convention Chairman, started by saying that the gospel is to the Jew *first*, and so introduced Hannah Hurnard, the first speaker, who spoke of the way in which Jewish people in Israel were now eager to receive and read the Scriptures as never before.

Years later, that young man wrote a poem expressing his love for Keswick, a poem quoted (in part) in the 1977 *Keswick Newsletter*.

But he wasn't to know that in years to come, he also would serve in the ranks of CMJ: the Church's Ministry among Jewish people, with whom Hannah worked, and would become a near neighbour of Marjorie Hurnard, Hannah's beloved stepmother. Today his work on behalf of God's covenant people, takes him to numerous churches in different countries, and includes the wonderful privilege of writing this tribute to Hannah's life and ministry.

The Things I Love

The tall straight trees
  By Buttermere,
The tents at Keswick
  Every year,
The mountains soaring
  Steep and high,
And sunset colours
  In the sky.

Soft springing turf
  In sunlit fields,
The gentle wavelets'
  White-flecked rills,
A Church's tall
  And stately spire,
An oak-beamed room,
  A blazing fire.

The lambs that grace
  The grassy hill,
And streams that feed
  A turning mill,
The lover's sweet
  And slender grace,
A mother's warm
  and tender face.

The Book of God,
  A stirring hymn,
The joy of simply
  Loving Him,
The bond that binds
  Our hearts as one,
The hope of heaven
  When all is done.

18 *Intercessors for Israel*

I

Even before she had left her beloved Galilee in 1951, Hannah realised that her visitation work was drawing to a close. That last lonely trip out to an Orthodox Jewish community, where she blushed to announce herself as an evangelist among Jewish people, because of what so-called Christian countries had done to God's covenant people, especially in recent times, had signalled the end of this particular phase in her ministry. Now she was to be a witness to the nations of what God was doing for His people, Israel.

The opportunity to do this presented itself sooner than she could have expected. In 1949, Hannah's relationships with her Swiss colleague, Lilly, had become strained because of Lilly's new charismatic emphasis. Being a good Quaker lady, Hannah had a mortal dread of all this 'speaking in tongues', and couldn't abide undue excitability in worship! But then came a totally unexpected letter from Lilly's Pentecostal mentor in Switzerland. He had heard about Hannah's ministry on behalf of Israel, and wanted her to visit a dozen Pentecostal churches in Switzerland on her way back to the Holy Land in the late summer of 1951. Would she be willing to do so?

Hannah's first reaction was to refuse. But a 'stop' in her mind prevented her from posting the letter. Shouldn't she pray for guidance about the whole matter first?

In the event, it was the story in Acts 10 of Peter being

required to eat all kinds of non-kosher food, to the horror of his Orthodox compatriots, that made her think again (v 15). She asked for three signs that it would be right for her to risk misunderstanding by others, as well as a measure of discomfort within herself (v 16), and when all three requests were duly granted within a matter of days, she sent her acceptance. How could she refuse to minister among fellow believers whom God had likewise cleansed?

A Swiss friend warned her that other churches in her country would close their doors to her if she persisted with her plans. But, as Matthew Henry once said, we should never doubt in the dark what God has told us in the light. So Hannah went ahead.

'The two weeks which I spent visiting the Pentecostal Assemblies turned out to be nothing but a blessing,' she later wrote. Then in words which she did not always find it easy to apply in subsequent theological conflicts, she added: 'I began to discover that it was the easiest thing in all the world to have happy fellowship with people with whom one totally disagrees on some matters, as long as one does not insist on airing one's own views and condemning others' (*The Opened Understanding*, pp 55, 56).

II

Meanwhile, on her last morning in England, Hannah had come down to breakfast to find a letter from New Zealand lying beside her plate. She noticed that it was in her sister-in-law's handwriting. What could be the matter? Why hadn't her brother Bracy written the letter?

Her fingers trembled as she slit open the envelope. Then she understood. Bracy's doctor feared that he was suffering from leukaemia, and while Bracy was not to be told, his wife Janet wanted Hannah to know the situation. It looked as though their four young sons would soon be fatherless.

As she flew to Zurich, Hannah's mind was in turmoil. She was glad to have ten days relaxing in the mountains before her series of meetings. It gave her time to reflect. Should she take time out to visit her brother in New Zealand? Clearly she was no expert in nursing. But then Janet herself was a trained nurse. In spite of her time spent as housekeeper in Jerusalem, Hannah still did not have the practical skills needed for looking after a family. So wouldn't she be in the way: a hindrance rather than a help in the home? And supposing she flew all that way, how long would she need to stay there? If she were in New Zealand too long, her Israeli Resident's visa would expire. And wouldn't Bracy smell a rat if his sister suddenly turned up, camping on his doorstep? In any case, she did not have enough money to pay for the air fare.

But as so often happens, Scripture and circumstance combined to confirm her inward conviction. Once back in Israel, she wandered down to the lakeside to celebrate the twentieth anniversary of her arrival in the Holy Land, and as the waters lapped around her, she imagined the Lord walking towards her along the shore, calling her to leave her nets and follow Him.

She realised that, in her case, the 'nets' were the car and caravan she was hoping to import. But on this January morning in 1952, at the age of forty-six, Hannah did not find it easy to think of leaving all she had come to love. She had deep emotional investments in the land where Jesus lived, and found it hard to step out, like Abraham, not knowing where she was going (Heb 11:8).

But Isaiah 49:2 had impressed itself on her mind some time before. She was to be an arrow hidden in God's quiver, ready to be sent from place to place, trusting the Lord to make her mouth like a sharp sword.

The next morning, Hannah received a letter from the Israeli Import Authority, telling her that because she had nowhere to live, they would permit her to import the caravan, but not the car. However, the English Customs had already refused her an export licence for the caravan, but were quite prepared to let her export the car to Israel!

It was all so ludicrous, Hannah quivered with laughter! But

at least the bungling bureaucracy settled the issue. Not having even a mobile home of her own in the land, left her no option. She would have to leave. Moreover, the money she had set aside to pay for the licences, would cover the cost of her flight.

So, after queueing up at the depot for a long time, Hannah was able to climb aboard the over-crowded bus, and stand strap-hanging for two-and-a-half hours as it lurched across potholed roads to Haifa, where she bought a one-way ticket for New Zealand. She was under no illusions. From now on, she was to be a person of 'no fixed abode'.

On her final day in Galilee, she had climbed the hill above Nazareth to take one last long look at the place where Jesus had spent his boyhood years. Suddenly, high in the sky, she had seen the wheeling battalions of storks, arriving for their annual migration, 'the sun flashing on their white wings as they circled lower and lower towards the green plains and the croaking frogs.'

On Good Friday 1952, Hannah also 'migrated', as she took the wings of the morning, and flew from Tel Aviv, across the wind-patterned deserts of Arabia, and the teeming villages of India, towards 'the land of the long white cloud', where one of her favourite authors, F.W. Boreham, had lived, and where her ailing brother now battled with his baffling illness.

III

After a three day stop-over in Sydney, Hannah flew on to Wellington in the North Island, where she sent a telegram to Janet and Bracy, telling them she was on her way, and would be landing at Christchurch on the South Island in no time at all!

To her surprise, Bracy was there to meet her. He had insisted on getting up and being driven to the airport with their four sons: John, Stuart, Brian, and Roger. The emergency Hannah had travelled so far to share, was over! Though never robust, Bracy nevertheless grew strong enough to found and run his own business in New Zealand, living on into his eighty-eighth year, and dying just eleven weeks before Hannah did in 1990. However, his wife Janet died of a heart attack while getting out of a car ten years earlier in May 1980.

But if Hannah could not be the dutiful sister and aunt she had counted on being during what she had thought would be Bracy's last days on earth, her arrival in New Zealand proved providential in other ways.

Hannah was the first Christian worker from the Holy Land to visit the Antipodes after the establishment of the State of Israel, and Christians everywhere were eager to learn all they could about the situation there. So Hannah was more than happy to share her news!

Since her retreat on Mount Olympus in Cyprus two years earlier, Hannah had gained even greater fluency in speech, and was much improved in health. So her diary soon filled up with appointments, her mouth was 'like a sharp sword', and many new intercessors for Israel were enlisted.

Unfortunately, there was a muddle over her books! Back in 1947 she had written an account of her evangelistic enterprises in the Holy Land. But no publisher had been prepared to bring it out, and when she tried to have it printed privately in England four years later, paper rationing made it impossible. However, Bracy had arranged to have 2,000 copies of *Wayfarer in the Land* printed in New Zealand, where paper was still available.

So far, so good! But Hannah had not told her brother she was coming to New Zealand, for fear of causing him anxiety. So he had promptly arranged to have the whole consignment of books sent by a slow boat to England, just before Hannah herself flew into New Zealand!

But the printer came to their rescue by running off another three hundred copies for her immediate use, while the delay in getting the main order back from England, gave her the chance to rethink her future plans.

With so many invitations reaching her from both Islands,

as well as from Australia, Hannah concluded that she was meant to cancel the boat ticket for England which she had already bought. But what was to happen about her Israeli visa? If she did not return there within a year, she would automatically lose the right to reside in the country.

It was a cruel dilemma. She yearned for the heavenly hills and lovely lake of Galilee. And she still hoped it might be possible to get her car and caravan into Israel. Years of serving among both Jews and Arabs had given her an abiding love for the people there. If home is where the heart is, then Israel was where she truly belonged.

But once again the decision was taken out of her hands. Although she was not in any way responsible for a debt that was incurred in printing 4,000 more copies of her book *Watchman on the Walls*, Hannah felt obliged to take the situation on board, and stay in the area until the whole problem was resolved.

In doing that, Hannah's clear call to raise up an army of intercessors for Israel was abundantly confirmed, and her soul was set singing by all the new glad experiences which came her way in so many different countries of the world.

IV

Hannah had a profound dislike of having her photograph taken. In fact any kind of publicity was anathema to her. Even when she became a best-selling author, she would never take part in any book signings. Consequently we have few photographic records of her remarkable career.

But her books and letters are full of vivid *word* pictures drawn from her globe-trotting ministry. In late 1952, for example, she visited the South Sea Islands, and wrote graphic little cameos of her canoeing among the coral reefs, or watching the grass-skirted islanders nursing their young.

In the little thatched churches of the Coral Islands, the children and grandchildren of former cannibals, sat enthralled as she told stories of Jesus which had happened in the very places where she had been living for twenty years.

One little Papuan girl, brought up on a mission compound, and able to speak some English, took Hannah's hand. 'Tell us what it is like in the home country of Jesus,' she said, being careful to translate Hannah's answer for the benefit of all the other girls strolling along with them in the sunshine. Then she looked up into Hannah's face very earnestly, and asked, 'Have you really seen Jesus over there? What is He like? I wish I could see Him too.'

Hannah spoke to the lepers on their isolated island as they sat in the open under a huge banyan tree round a table spread with a white cloth one Sunday morning. Her words about the Saviour stretching out His hands to a disobedient and rebellious people (Rom 10:21), touched the heart of one man in particular. 'One of the hardest trials of our life on this leper island is the fact that there seems so little we can do for the Lord Jesus,' he said to her. 'But now, in His loving kindness He has sent you from His home country to ask us to pray for the salvation of His own kinspeople, the Jews. Some of us are now going to make this our special service for Him.'

It is possible to imagine all kinds of privations suffered by people suffering from Hansen's Disease. But lacking the opportunity to render practical service for Christ would probably not rank very high on any list of priorities we might compile. Yet that was precisely the loss he and his friends felt most keenly as Hannah ministered among them that day.

Such positive experiences amply compensated her for the pain of giving up her prized privilege of being an Israeli resident. 'How little I thought, away there on the hilltop of Nazareth,' she wrote on her second autobiography, 'that enlisting intercessors would be such a joyful ministry' (pp 77, 78).

19 The Making of Books

From the second year of her discipleship, Hannah learned to pray on paper! Perhaps it was because she still found it difficult to communicate verbally, that she resorted to writing out her devotions. I know that in my own experience, partial deafness when I was young tended to cut me off from other people, including some members of my own family, and drove me to articulate my ideas in written form. I can *still* argue better on paper than in person!

At any rate, Hannah found that nearly all the spiritual illumination and guidance she received, came as she wrote, rather than as she prayed either audibly or silently. Jennifer Rees Larcombe in our own day, has confessed to a similar kind of devotional life.

It seemed to Hannah that in the very act of writing down her reflections on a passage of Scripture, or the pros and cons of any particular course of action, every issue was clarified, new insights were given, and the way forward was made plain. For many Christians, including myself, the use of a daily Prayer Diary, fulfils a similar function.

On top of all this, of course, Hannah was an inveterate letter-writer. Every week she wrote home, first to her father, then after 1949, to her stepmother Marjorie. When working in FEB, she produced an occasional newsletter to send out to her prayer partners: a practice she continued from time to time when serving with the British Jews Society in Haifa.

Moreover, as a Christian worker, whether in FEB or BJS, Hannah was required to produce regular written reports on her work to send to her overseers. So, without her realising what was happening, Hannah was steadily being trained to become a Christian writer.

Hannah was always an *intense* person. She pondered things deeply, and felt them keenly. She also possessed an insatiable curiosity about life in general, and was a close observer of human nature. As a writer, she was a natural.

The fact that she had been steeped in the cadences of the Authorised Version (KJV) from childhood, meant that her literary tastes were shaped and measured by the highest possible standards. From the outset she revelled in Bunyan's *Pilgrim's Progress*. Later she read widely in biography, popular theology, devotional literature, and the Mystics. As both her father and mother, as well as her paternal grandfather, were gifted writers, it is hardly surprising that Hannah should also have put pen to paper in 'the making of books'.

II

There is no doubt at all that it was during the fifties that Hannah's creative gifts as a writer reached full flower. In all, she wrote twelve books in ten years. Not all of them were of the same high standard, of course. Even Homer nods. But three in particular have stood the test of time: *The Hearing Heart*, her first biography; *Watchman on the Walls*, based on the journal she kept during the War of Independence (1948 – 1950); and *Hinds' Feet on High Places*, her spiritual classic.

Hannah's method was to write out each manuscript in what she once described as 'an incredibly dreadful scrawl' which only she could decipher! Then she would type it all up on her ancient machine, laboriously picking out the letters one by one, using only three fingers! Once the manuscript was parcelled up and posted off, there was the inevitable and seemingly interminable wait for the publisher's reply. She had no literary agent!

Like most aspiring writers, Hannah received her fair share of rejection slips. It didn't help that some of her attempts to be published coincided with the Second World War and the years of austerity in Britain which followed immediately afterward. Even so, there were several publishers who lived to rue the day they turned down this unknown lady writer who lived and worked in the distant country of Palestine, with which Christian relationships have always been somewhat ambivalent.

In the event, it was the publishing arm of CMJ, Olive Press, which brought out her very first book in January 1950: *Watchman on the Walls*. With but the briefest mention in the Society's in-house magazine, the first edition sold out in no time at all, and several reprints followed. As part of her dedication to the Lord Jesus Christ, and out of gratitude towards the Society she served with such distinction, Hannah donated all the royalties for this and six subsequent books to CMJ, the Church's Ministry among Jewish people, as it is now called. Only the proceeds from *The Unveiled Glory*, the book she published privately in 1956 to explain her theological position, were retained for her own use now that she had begun to live without financial support from other sources.

III

Like an artist setting up his easel on the hillside to paint some stunning landscape, Hannah would gather up her Bible and 'Quiet Time' notebooks, make for some strategic vantage point, soak up the surrounding scenery, and pour out her heart on to the pristine pages of her latest manuscript.

How she gloried in the colour-rich warmth and beauty of nature! During the First World War, her father had kept some little brown rabbits in the paddock at Hill House, to supplement their meagre wartime rations. But he had also given Hannah a special big, snowy-white, pink-eyed rabbit to be her very own pet. When tired of human company, and frustrated with her inability to communicate, Hannah would take her pet Peter out of his hutch, cuddle him close, and feel his long white ears twitching gently against her cheek. For the whole of one beautiful long summer, she took special delight in his company, as he in hers. He came whenever she called his name, and followed her like Mary's little lamb! She called it 'A Garden of Eden friendship'.

On 18th March, 1938, Hannah's letter home described the joy she found in tending some plants in her little apartment down in the Jewish quarter of Haifa.

> My balcony garden is lovely just now. I have ten pots of bulbs either in flower or in bud, as well as carnations, freesias, and geraniums, and some wonderful arum lilies – three flowers on one plant. The unprecedented amount of rain this winter has made the country look glorious, and even the balcony has blossomed like the rose.

Those who know her book, *Hinds' Feet on High Places*, are familiar with the foreword where she describes the view from her window when she lived, on what we now know as the West Bank, during the forties.

> From the garden at the back of the Mission House at the foot of Mount Gerizim, we could often watch the gazelles bounding up the mountain-side, leaping from rock to rock with extraordinary grace and agility.

It called to mind the description of the Shepherd-lover, the Lord Jesus, 'leaping upon the mountains, skipping upon the hills' (Song 2:8, KJV). As the smiling Arab nurse explained when they read that passage one day, 'there are no obstacles which our Saviour's love cannot overcome.'

Hannah was to discover the truth of that insight during the War of Independence in 1948. Surrounded by the sight of wounded patients in the Jerusalem Hospital, and the stench of rotting corpses in nearby caves, Hannah's heart would suddenly be lifted by the sun-bathed glory of hibiscus flowers and blue delphiniums blossoming in the hospital flower beds.

Danger was all around them. One day Hannah's friend

Lilly was shaken by bullets embedding themselves into the wall above her head. Hannah herself dodged shells when feeding the hens Jemima and Keren in the compound. But then, watching the porcupine quills of the ugly little pigeon babies unfurl into feathers before her very eyes one day, sent a surge of excitement through her.

> All these things, and countless others, especially the kindness and goodness of Ruth (Clark), Ronald (Adeney), Lilly and Mrs Gibson, give a pleasure and content and active delight, I have never before experienced, just by the very contrast to the horrors around' (she wrote). 'One Sunday, while we were at Communion, my eyes kept straying through the open door into the garden, where the sun was shining hotly on the tree beside the gate house, gilding the bare trunk and the dry earth with glory, and it gave me a thrill every time.

IV

Each book Hannah wrote was a child born into the world at some lovely location. On Mount Olympus in Cyprus in 1950, she wrote *The Secret of a Transformed Thought Life*. Later that same year, she sat by the shores of Galilee eagerly writing her beautifully scripted life story: *The Hearing Heart*.

When in May 1953, Hannah took her leave of New Zealand, and flew to Canada, she lodged by the side of a lake and wrote her Testament: *The Kingdom of Love*.

In early 1954, after finding great enjoyment in exploring Manhattan Island and the United Nations Headquarters in New York, she produced her fascinating little book on prayer: *God's Transmitters*, in which she argued that the person who lives and prays in God, emits powerful signals for good into lives and situations that are plagued by harm.

After visiting the West Indies that year to continue enlisting intercessors for Israel, Hannah took a long six week vacation in Switzerland during the summer. While there, she wrote both *Hinds' Feet* and *Mountains of Spices* with their vivid evocation of alpine scenery.

She gave the script of *Hinds' Feet* to her dearest friend, Marjorie, to vet. At the time, Marjorie was busy running Hill House, and had to wait until she got to bed at night before she could bury herself in Hannah's beautiful story. But she recognised at once that there was something very special about this book, and urged Hannah to publish it. 'I owe *Hinds' Feet* to Marjorie,' Hannah used to say.

But paradoxically, it was shortly after this, and just when Dr Billy Graham's Crusades had taken London by storm, bringing new vigour to evangelical life throughout the whole of Britain, that Hannah told Marjorie of her new understanding of the gospel. The news rocked her back on her heels. It seemed hard to believe that her honoured stepdaughter was beginning to move away from some of those convictions which had hitherto motivated her life and ministry. Yet it is typical of this remarkable woman, that she allowed no theological differences to disrupt her loving and loyal support for Hannah. Whenever problems arose in subsequent days, it was to Hill House and her most gracious stepmother that Hannah invariably returned.

In her later years, when dividing her time between Israel and Essex, Hannah delighted to stay in her mobile home on Mersea Island. Then on Saturday mornings, she would drive into Colchester to go shopping. After that she would call at 7 Elianore Road, Lexden, where Marjorie lived from 1967 onwards. Her last entry in Marjorie's visitors book, written in Hannah's self-confessed scrawl, reads 'With loving gratitude for forty-eight years of loving kindness and friendship, 31st August, 1984'.

As a girl, Hannah had appreciated the views from Mersea Island across the estuary to Bradwell, where England's oldest church still being used for worship, stands astride the remnants of an old Roman sea wall and fort. Now, in her mature years, she would sit gazing out to sea, meditating on her ever-widening vision of God's fathomless love, and writing half-yearly booklets to give away to praying friends. Her proofreader, aptly named Mr Partner, Peter and Betty Taylor who were former workers at Hill House, and Daphne English the cook, like so many other people in Colchester and beyond, still treasure those seaside offerings.

Eventually Hannah exchanged the caravan, which could be rather cold and damp under certain English conditions, for a delightful little cottage only a few yards away, which she named 'Galilee'. There, for six months of each year, she worked among the children who were taking their summer holidays on the island, and continued her writing ministry, until in 1984, she finally moved to America, and Marjorie saw her no more.

20 Closing the Door behind Her

I

Towards the end of her second autobiography, Hannah appeared to dismiss her early work in Israel as inconsequential. There have been other missionaries who have similarly regarded their former ministry as worthless once they came into what they imagined to be an altogether higher state of spirituality. But that was not necessarily the way others saw it. At the end of the day, we have to leave the final assessment of our work to a higher mind than ours.

> It was the chief sorrow of my life as a missionary in Palestine (she wrote) that with all the zeal and sincere desire to make the Lord Jesus known to others, I seemed so powerless to awaken any desire for Him in the hearts of other people. Even the few 'converts' did not seem to make real and vital and transforming contact with His power, but always seemed disappointed with the results and experiences which followed their costly change over from Judaism to Christianity (p 172).

There are times in the lives of all who are involved in Christian service, when they feel themselves to be failures. Hannah was not the first or the last missionary to experience a sense of deep disappointment. How little we seem to achieve for the One who wrought so much for us! But the final chapter of our life's story has not yet been written. Nor do we know what fruit the former chapters might *yet* produce for the Kingdom of Heaven.

In contrast to Hannah's rather gloomy assessment of her work in Israel, an advertisement for BJS in 1936 quoted from one of Hannah's own letters, describing the reaction of one Jewish woman to whom she had witnessed.

> She rushed home and poured it all out to her husband (Hannah wrote). He was very angry, and by and by she came to me and said: 'My husband says the missionaries have influenced me and that I must shut my eyes. But how can I shut them now they begin to be opened? I must tell you today I have realised how happy you all are in your faith and how real God is to you. WE HAVE NOTHING LIKE IT IN JUDAISM. It must be lovely to feel that you are working for God. I must tell you today that it is not a little thing that has happened to me today, but a very great experience.'

Anyone witnessing to Jewish people has to recognise that there is a veil over the hearts of unbelieving Jews, so that their eyes are kept from recognising Jesus as Messiah (Luke 24:16). It is only when He Himself draws near and opens their minds to understand the Scriptures (v 45), that the veil is removed and the truth is revealed.

Hannah worked among Jewish people just when all the centuries of anti-Jewish feelings among Christian people reached their climax in the horrors of the holocaust, and when the so-called Christian governments of the time, including our own, were failing the Jewish people at almost every point. Is it at all surprising, therefore, that Hannah and her fellow-workers saw so little response to their witness?

The situation now is very different. Since the establishment of the State of Israel in 1948, numerous Jewish books and articles about Jesus have struck a very positive note. There is a lively and flourishing department in the Hebrew University at Jerusalem, which specialises in the study of the New Testament. And in the twenty years since 1975, the number of Messianic congregations throughout Israel, has grown from five to more than forty, and far from changing over from Judaism to Christianity, as Hannah put it, their members maintain their Jewishness very strongly, while embracing Y'shua as their Messiah.

II

In the summer of 1936, Hannah stayed as a paying guest in the home of a delightful Orthodox Jewish couple in Jerusalem, so that she could learn a little more conversational Hebrew.

She proved an excellent 'Shabbas goy' for the five or six weeks she lived with them. They were not allowed to turn on the lights or use the cooker once the ram's horn had announced the start of Shabbat just before sunset on Fridays, nor could they request Hannah to do so. But by noting the times when special foods had to be prepared for their little baby, who was being weaned, and by being careful to switch the lights on and off as and when necessary, thus saving the couple heavy fuel bills, the normally impractical Hannah rendered invaluable service to them. She was also able to help the couple with their English, just as they were daily helping her with her Hebrew.

Inevitably, when each day drew to a close, they would engage in conversation and dialogue. It mystified them that Hannah should debase herself by being a 'missionary'. The very word is anathema to a good Jew because of the way Christian missions have so often divided whole families in years gone by. But while that particular challenge to her calling gave Hannah the opportunity to witness to 'the greatest Jew who ever lived', she was totally unprepared for the young man's searing reply to her. 'But supposing people do not believe in him because they genuinely consider him to have been a blasphemer?' he asked, to her obvious discomfort. Then, when she explained that unbelief always results in spiritual loss, he avowed that there was no way he could believe in a God who brought countless souls into the world, and then consigned them to endless punishment because He was unable to stop them repudiating Him.

Hannah was stunned by his trenchant argument, and as it came at a time when she was still smarting over her father's decision to marry a woman six-and-a-half years younger than herself, and from an altogether lowlier background, she was feeling more than a little vulnerable. So the young man's words took root in her mind.

III

A few years later, while living in Beisan, and visiting local settlements in the company of an Arab nurse, Hannah was involved in a most harrowing experience, which eventually affected her thinking quite dramatically.

A young woman in that comparatively primitive area, where sanitation was poor, and medical facilities meagre, had just given birth to a baby, but because of complications, she was now in a desperate condition. Night had fallen, the roads were bad, and terrorism was rampant. But Hannah agreed to drive the nurse and her patient to Nazareth Hospital, just over thirty-five kilometres away.

They drove without headlights for most of the journey, until they reached the twisting mountain road leading up to the town. By now the woman was unconscious, and her terrified young husband was beside himself with anguish. Hannah and the nurse did their best to find a piece of iron to force between the clenched teeth of the dying woman. At the same time, they tried to console the frantic husband, while caring for the two-hour-old child. But no sooner had the patient been taken through the hospital doors on a stretcher, and laid on the operating table, than she breathed her last.

Hannah was totally devastated. Their journey had been in vain. The girl had died without hearing the gospel. And they felt powerless to minister any comfort to the desperate man.

Next morning, they drove back to Beisan, the young man clutching his beloved's body, begging her, with every possible endearment, to speak to him. On the outskirts of the town, he collected two spades for the digging of her grave. The two women left him at his peasant cottage with heavy hearts.

As she pondered the incident again and again in later years, Hannah became convinced that as surely as the Lord had been with them as they drove through that dark and dangerous night on their errand of mercy, so surely He was with the dying Muslim woman as she slipped into eternity.

IV

After the traumas in Jerusalem's War of Independence, Hannah found sanctuary on Mount Olympus in Cyprus (1950). As the days slipped by in fellowship with the Lord, remote from every care and responsibility, the tensions eased away from her, and she was filled with 'boundless charity divine'. It was like a second conversion.

Years before, she had read and rejected a book which spoke of the Suffering God who is so closely identified with His whole creation, that He bears the endless pain of man's rejection. Now, in 'the Kingdom of Love', she came to accept that same conviction. The God who embraces all men in the arms of His love with patient compassion, was allowing her to share in His wounded heart and forgivingness.

All her life long, she had found it easy to recognise the undesirable traits in other people. Even her prayers had tended to become inventories of their weaknesses, duly recited before the Lord in the pious hope that He would enable them to change! Now she realised the need to be transformed by the renewing of her *own* mind, and to see her critical attitude for what it was: a denial of that Kingdom Love she was now tasting in her heart.

Up there, on 'the borderline of the High Places', she had found the love which says: 'It is happy to love, even if you are not loved in return; it is happy to serve, even if the service is not appreciated; it is happy to give, even if what is given is taken for granted or nothing is given in return; it is happy to forgive, even if you are wronged again and again.'

As time went by, Hannah's questing spirit took delight in a whole new area of devotional literature which reinforced this emphasis. At the doctor's house in Tiberias later that year, she devoured the writings of A.J. Gossip, George MacDonald, and C.S. Lewis. In New Zealand, a taciturn young man at the Christian guest house where she was staying in early 1953, introduced her to *The Spirit of Love*, a book of pithy extracts from the writings of William Law, whose works had strongly influenced John Wesley.

Once back in England, after a visit to Israel in 1955, ostensibly to dispose of some belongings there, she discovered a kindred spirit in Evelyn Underhill, and began to immerse herself in the writings of many other fellow mystics.

Meanwhile, she had concluded that far too many evangelical Christians were as hidebound in their orthodoxy, and as resistant to new light, as the Pharisees had been. Her own adventurous spirit was eager to explore every possible avenue of spiritual enlightenment, and being the kind of person she was, she could never keep silent about all the new penetrating insights which her mystical experiences gave to her. As she said in a letter to me, written when she was a lively eight-three years of age:

> We can't unsee what we have seen,
> But ask God to show more,
> And lead us on to richer truths
> Than we could see before.
> His love will teach our still dimmed eyes,
> And we shall come to see
> More of His wondrous love and grace
> Through all eternity.

V

In late 1955, Hannah visited each of the eight countries in Central America to enlist more intercessors for Israel, before going on to the United States in readiness for a conference to be held in January 1956.

But by now, Hannah was bursting to share with all and sundry about her new conception of God's universal love, and this emphasis was beginning to eclipse everything else. In fact she felt it was quite useless to ask Christian people to pray in love for Israel, when they refused to practise true one-ness among themselves.

Moreover, she had become convinced that hitherto she had only ever preached half a gospel, for she now believed beyond any shadow of doubt, that 'the Saviour will win a final and complete victory, and will win over every single human soul and false spirit to love Him of their own free will.' No argument, or plea for caution, was allowed to stop her shouting this vision from the rooftop!

Once in the States, she was encouraged to share her views in a house group, when her hostess felt led to draw her attention to Esther 4:14. If Hannah did not speak out about her vision, then God would find someone else ready and willing to do so. However, once her hostess had actually heard what Hannah had to say, she got cold feet, and wondered whether it might have been a 'deceiving spirit' which had urged her to pass on that particular text to her!

Hannah herself was distressed by the reaction to her address that day, and took refuge in her old habit of opening the Bible at random. Sure enough, the well-thumbed Bible fell open at 1 Samuel 3:15,18, where, after being reluctant to tell old Eli what God had revealed to him, young Samuel eventually 'hid nothing from him' (KJV). Then neither would Hannah! She seemed oblivious to the fact that whereas Samuel's message had been one of stern judgment, her own was quite the opposite!

It was inevitable that her universalist teaching would cause a clash at the Conference she had been asked to address. As she said herself, the delegates were keen Bible students who wanted to know how prophecy was being ful-filled in the Middle East. Instead (with the leaders' permission), Hannah was communicating her 'Kingdom of Love' teaching, which urged believers to reach out, in unjudging acceptance, to all and sundry, whatever their theological views, as surely as the heavenly Father does.

The reaction was entirely predictable. Her emphasis on 'oneness' caused division. And once the news got round, as it was bound to do, her other appointments were cancelled, and some of her publications were withdrawn. It was an agonising time for her, and she fell ill with what one doctor suspected was cancer. Some intense Christians regarded this illness as God's judgment on her error.

However, one of her hearers caught something of her breathtaking vision of God's omnipotent love, and sent a copy of her book, *The Winged Life*, to Dr Glenn Clark, founder of Camps Farthest Out.

In 1939, this Harvard graduate, successful athletics coach, high school principal, and popular writer, had asked for 300 volunteers to form a Gideon's Band, prepared to adventure in prayer with courage and faith. Eventually, after a visit to Monhegan Island, which was called 'the island farthest out', he planned a number of camps where Christians could set up prayer laboratories, and explore 'the realm farthest out': God's Kingdom of love and power. Hence the name of his movement.

After reading Hannah's little book, Glenn Clark travelled out to see the ailing Hannah in California, on what was to be one of his last expeditions. His words of counsel and encouragement did her good. Not only did she recover from the illness, which had been caused by stress, the door opened for her to speak at CFO conferences. So her empty diary filled up, and her financial needs were met. Moreover, she was able to enjoy a rich experience of loving acceptance, which brought healing to her heart.

VI

There were times when Hannah was tempted to accuse evangelicals of being so unwilling to open their minds to new truth, that they effectively frustrated her calling to communicate the Kingdom of Love ministry which she believed the Lord had given her. And there can be no doubt that, when writing critical letters, some Christians are capable of considerable venom once roused to unrighteous indignation! She never found it easy to cope with some of the spiteful communications she received.

But she was never less than honest. By 1955, when she had first broached the matter to Marjorie, she realised that she would eventually need to close the door behind her. 'I knew that to obey the new commission which I had received from the Lord on Mount Zion, and to begin to bear witness to my new beliefs, I must literally go "outside the camp", that is outside the circle of Christian fellowship in doctrine and belief in which I had been nurtured,' she wrote in her second autobiography (p 130).

Less than a year later she was telling Glenn Clark that she was 'happy and thankful to have jumped over the wall and gone outside the camp into real freedom to share all the glorious illumination God was giving her,' though she was baffled to know why there were so few opportunities for doing so (*Thou Shalt Remember*, p 139).

She was a woman of integrity. So, having written an explanatory letter in America, she returned to England in the summer of 1956, to write a book answering some of the objections to her views which had been voiced at the Conference in America earlier that year. She also sent out yet another circular letter for the benefit of all her friends and associates in the United Kingdom, even though she knew that this letter, like the earlier one, would yet again close the door behind her.

That newsletter is before me as I write. Like *The Unveiled Glory* which explains her views at greater length, it is a powerful and persuasive exposition of her 'larger hope', and draws attention to any number of Scripture passages which it is easy for Christian people to gloss over when discussing these matters.

Nevertheless, it is not free from special pleading, especially when, in dealing with those verses in Revelation which speak about 'the lake of fire', she adds: 'We need to remember that fire is always a symbol for Holy Love', as though such a statement, which is itself open to question, could possibly justify her belief that devils as well as sinners, will ultimately become lovers of holiness. It is *destruction*, and not conversion, which those verses manifestly teach (Rev 20:11-15; 21:5-8).

It is one of the strange ironies of Hannah's story, that while her father left the local Quaker Meeting because of its increasing liberalism, and became an outright evangelical, Hannah herself closed the door on her evangelical background in becoming a theological liberal.

21 To the Law and the Testimony

Those who are privileged to work among God's covenant people, the Jews, never cease to thank God for all they have received from the common roots they share with Jewish people.

It is true that modern Judaism is more Rabbinic than Scriptural. But both Jews and Christians are meant to be 'people of the Book'. Moreover, they share the same root, because Messiah is 'the root and the offspring of David' (Rev 22:16, KJV), and they are nourished by the same sap: the ongoing grace of God (Rom 11:17,18).

What is so frustrating about all this is that while the kinship between Jews and Christians is so close, the distance between them is often so great. If it is difficult to enable Jewish people to understand why we are so convinced that Y'shua is Messiah, it is equally hard to persuade Christians to recover their kinship with the blood brothers of Jesus.

There are historical reasons for this situation, and, as in so many areas of Christian witness, we need more patience, understanding and love than we have shown hitherto.

Yet we can take heart from the way in which many Christians are beginning to realise how the Church's attitude towards Jews in the past, has been responsible for so much anti-semitism. Moreover, there is now a greater respect for the person of Jesus among both religious and secular Jews, than there has ever been.

Hannah met Jewish people who put the principles of Jesus into practice more than many Christians did. And Professor David Flusser of the Hebrew University in Jerusalem, has been heard to say, with typical chutzpah (cheek), that he is more New Testament in his theology than some Christian scholars are!

Again and again, when meeting wonderfully open, devout and upright Jewish people, or reading those insightful books and articles about Jesus written by Jewish people, we echo the words of Jesus, when he said to a Torah Teacher of His times: 'You are not far from the Kingdom of Heaven.'

There are Biblical Christians who believe, with Paul, that the true olive branches which have been broken off because of unbelief, will be grafted back in, 'and so all Israel shall be saved' (Rom 11:26).

As she watched events unfold in Israel, Hannah came to see that God still has His hand on His people. He has certainly not abandoned them. Least of all have Christians somehow replaced them. Her father had understood all this long before, of course. But now it was becoming real to Hannah herself, because she was actually on the spot when so many of the prophecies Samuel had highlighted were coming true. In fact she was part of the whole extraordinary event.

Yet Israel's return to the land is not enough. That is only one half of God's promise to His people. The greater half is still to follow. Scripture calls on us to pray for Israel's full restoration to the Lord Himself, when, in enjoyment of the new covenant, both Israel and Judah will experience God's forgiving grace, receive His indwelling Spirit, and know God for themselves (Jer 31:31-34; Ezek 36:24-28).

II

Clearly the relationship between devout Jews and Christians is unique. Jesus was an observing Jew, the Jewish Bible constitutes the larger part of the Christian Scriptures, and the Church began as a totally Jewish body. Nowadays, Jewish people who believe in Y'shua as Messiah insist that they are to be regarded, not as 'converted', but as 'completed' Jews.

But what about devotees of other faiths? At a time when relationships between different world religions are strengthening in some quarters, and inter-faith worship is sometimes taking place in Church buildings, this is becoming increasingly important.

When we turn to the New Testament, we soon discover that the apostles did not go out of their way to attack the many religions which flourished all around them. Indeed, they recognised that there were elements of truth in them, because, as Paul put it in his message to the people of Lystra: God has 'not left Himself without witness' (KJV) among those who had never known the direct revelation which Jews and Christians claim to know (Acts 14:17).

In his letter to the Romans, Paul made it clear that even pagans have an innate conception of God's power and deity. They can see Him at work in His creation. Moreover, they have an in-built conscience which makes them aware of right and wrong. At the end of the day they will be judged, not by the light they do not have, but by the light they do (Rom 1:19; 2:14-16).

In his letters to the young churches, Paul did not hesitate to use words and phrases familiar to adherents of other faiths: terms like 'illumination', 'wisdom', 'mystery' and 'sacrifice'. While at Athens, he used the inscription on a heathen altar nearby as the text for his sermon, even declaring that in worshipping 'the unknown God', they were in fact worshipping the Christians' God, albeit in ignorance (Acts 17:23).

The great apostle to the Gentiles did not hesitate to quote from pagan poets and playwrights with approval (Acts 17:28). Indeed, in Titus 1:12,13 he actually calls one of them a 'prophet', and confirms his witness as 'true'! With all the daring of faith, Paul explored the world of other religions, utilising their best insights, and demonstrating the fulfilment of all their fragmented understanding in the person of Jesus Christ, who is the Light which lightens every man (John 1:9).

Paul knew the dangers in all this, since he recognised that while idols are nonentities in themselves, the demons have nevertheless captured pagan religions for their own ends. So he called on Christians to stand apart from all association with pagan rites (2 Cor 6:16). There is no justification in the New Testament for inter-faith 'worship'. Quite the reverse.

Yet he proclaimed a cosmic Christ, who is 'the firstborn over all creation', and the One in whom all things hang together (Col 1:16,17). Moreover, He is destined to reconcile to Himself everything on earth and in heaven (Col 1:20). He holds the keys to death and the world beyond (Rev 1:18). He is Lord of all.

III

But does all this up-beat hope of Christ's on-going rule and end-time triumph mean that everyone will therefore experience final salvation, as Hannah insisted?

Originally she showed little interest in the whole sweep of early Church history, so she was probably quite unaware at first, that the great Christian scholar, Origen, had anticipated her viewpoint seventeen centuries before!

Origen is venerated as one of the greatest minds of the early Church, writing commentaries on every book of the Bible, teaching with consummate skill, and living as one whose life was 'one continuous act of prayer'. Although he came from Alexandria in Egypt, he also spent time working in the Holy Land. He likewise believed that God would eventually restore the whole created order, including Satan himself, to a perfect state. (See *New Dictionary of Theology*, IVP, 1988, p 702). His views were not finally rejected by the Church at large until some 300 years later.

Hannah confessed herself to be a 'mystic'. Like an impressionist painter, her mind intuitively grasped some wonderful insight, and felt it with such certainty, that she could only express it with compelling authority. But just as the onlooker does not always share the artist's vision, so many of

Hannah's hearers could not easily accept her new understanding. Hence we find her saying in her second autobiography:

> People were so concerned to have me taken out of the way because I believed that in the end God was going to change what I had always sorrowfully believed would be a sweeping victory for the Devil, into such a final and complete victory for the Saviour, that not one soul would continue to love evil, and even the Devil himself, would change into a lover of holiness (pp 146,147).

As always, it is so difficult to answer someone who says 'this is what the Lord has revealed to me.' Who are we to call into question another person's divine revelation? Yet we believe that it is wrong to interpret everything, including Scripture, in the light of our experience. Rather we must interpret experience in the light of Scripture. At the end of the day, we have to submit everything to the judgment of God's Word as honestly as we can, trusting that in so doing, we do not misunderstand what the Holy Spirit Himself is wanting to say to us through Scripture.

We are concerned to search out 'the whole counsel of God', taking into account *everything* that the Bible has to say on a given subject, and not relying on carefully selected texts which leave out those passages which do not fit into any pet theory we might hold. With the best will in the world, we cannot set aside or reinterpret much in the New Testament which clearly contradicts Hannah's conclusions.

An article by Hannah's mother, Rose, which is reproduced here, takes the whole question of divine judgment very seriously, and shows how Christ died *'the just for the unjust, that He might bring us to God'* (1 Pet 3:18, KJV). It certainly does not belittle the gravity of human sin, which is always self-destructive.

Hannah emphasised the Cross as expressing at one point of time, the on-going love of God which is always suffering man's wrong-doing, and always forgiving him. But in stressing the *universality* of the Cross, she was in danger of obscuring its *uniqueness*. His death at a particular time and place in history, accomplished the redemption of mankind in a radical, once-for-all kind of way. The Cross is pivotal. Everything literally hinges upon it. It is, as Jesus said, the judgement (Greek: *krisis*) of this world. It is the time and place where the Prince of this world is evicted, and his captives released, so that gentiles, as well as Jews, are now drawn to the One crowned King on His Cross (John 12:20f,31f).

The task of the Christian is not to argue in favour of one religion as against another, least of all to convince the world about the truth of 'Christianity'. It is to confront men and women with the person of Jesus and the power of His Cross. For 'we don't go around preaching about ourselves, but about Christ Jesus as Lord. All we say of ourselves is that we are your slaves because of what Jesus has done for us' (2 Cor 4:5, Living Bible).

But while this gospel is a savour of life to those who are being saved, we have to reckon with the fact that it is a stench of death to those who, by their unbelief, are 'perishing' (2 Cor 2:15f). For 'this is the verdict: Light has come into the world, but men loved darkness instead of light, because their deeds were evil,' Jesus said (John 3:19). In finally rejecting Christ, a person ultimately presses the self-destruct button.

Jesus warned that there is a broad road which leads down to perdition, and that even professing Christians stand in danger of His rejection if in fact they have no living relationship with Him. His hearers were solemnly urged to fear the one who has power to destroy both body and soul in hell. And He made it clear that those who disowned Him before men, would be disowned by Him before God (Matt 7:13f,21-23; 10:28,32-34).

Beyond such awesome solemnities, it would be irresponsible to speculate.

22 *Hannah's Legacy*

I

In early 1957, Hannah settled down to write her splendid little book on the beatitudes: *The Heavenly Powers*. Then in April she set out on a six month tour of America, taking in a number of house meetings and Camps Farthest Out.

While in the States, Hannah fell in with groups of other people who were also studying the mystics, and read more widely in this fertile field of spiritual experience. Moreover, she was now developing a keen interest in what can only be described as the 'paranormal'. Not that she was ever into anything 'black'. She was simply curious as to how spirit forces work. She recognised the danger all this presented. But she wanted to go beyond the merely 'psychic' to the genuinely spiritual. For her, Jesus alone was the one true 'medium'.

But none of this endeared her to her erstwhile friends. Letters continued to arrive expressing reactions varying from dismay to disgust. She patiently explained that it was still vital to share the good news, and to warn men and women about the terrors of hell. But there was little she could say to ameliorate the hurt so many trusting friends felt at being let down so badly by one they had revered so highly. Some wrote to say that they could never read anything she ever wrote again.

Hannah felt deeply upset by all this. So perhaps her 'Self' was not as dead as she imagined? Maybe her critics were right to say that she was in danger of self-idolatry. And when she arrived in New Zealand in October 1957 to find the atmosphere there distinctly chilly compared with previous visits, she had to admit that because of the adulation she had received in America, Self had indeed become puffed up once more.

Being free from speaking engagements for two months, gave Hannah the opportunity to write another book, *The Inner Man*. Then some groups in the North Island, who were interested in Camps Farthest Out, invited her to speak to them. So she was soon back on the teaching trail again.

By now she was thinking in terms of 'house group' ministry. She called such get-togethers 'Ulpans', the word used to describe Hebrew language schools in Israel. Her desire was to go about from place to place, sharing her Kingdom teaching with eager groups of 'disciples', who would then go out to influence other people, and to establish new Ulpan groups.

In a thinly disguised side-swipe at the kind of mass evangelism which was popular just then, Hannah pointed out that this method of going unannounced to small groups of people, with no advance publicity, no huge budgets, and no 'write ups' in the press, or lobbying of the rich and famous, was much more in accord with that used in New Testament times, and was infinitely preferable.

By April 1958, she was back in the States, putting all this into practice. But then in the summer of 1960, when feeling very tired after so much travelling and teaching, she went to stay with an ardent vegetarian in the mountains of New Mexico, and once again there followed yet another strange twist in her tale!

II

Hannah's hostess promised no hard sell when it came to vegetarianism. In fact her husband was still a meat-eater, and Hannah was perfectly free to share his menu, if she so wished. All the same, she put a little booklet on the subject alongside Hannah's breakfast the next morning, and it worked the oracle!

Mind you, when it came to vegetarianism, Hannah needed little persuasion. How could she ever forget that awful day during the First World War, when the meat rations had run out, and her pet rabbit, Peter, had disappeared from his hutch, only to turn up in the steaming dish on the dinner table that evening? With horror and outrage she had fled in tears from the table, and was utterly inconsolable.

Then, when living on the West Bank in the early 1940s, she had once witnessed the Samaritan Passover festivities on Mount Gerizim, near her home. When night fell, the High Priest had given the signal for each family to seize and slaughter its paschal lamb. As she watched the orgy of killing and feasting that night, she had turned away in revulsion from the whole squalid scene, her heart throbbing and pounding with unspeakable horror.

Now she came to believe that in giving His people permission to eat meat, God was in fact making a concession to their debased desires. According to Isaiah 1:11-15, she argued, God took no delight in His peoples' sacrifices at all. Yet neither Jews nor Christians seemed to have heeded such condemnations of ritual killing.

You would never have convinced Hannah that such passages meant that God disapproved of those sacrifices which were not accompanied by repentance, justice, obedience and honesty in the hearts and lives of His worshippers. Had God not manifestly instituted the whole sacrificial system spelt out in the Scriptures and fulfilled at the Cross?

When visiting the Pentecostal Assemblies in Switzerland, Hannah had concluded that, even when they disagree over some theological issues, Christians do not need to fall out with each other, provided they do not insist on airing their own views, or condemning the views of others. But once she had come to see that God originally intended mankind to be vegetarian (Gen 1:29), she lost no time in spreading the word with evangelistic urgency, in spite of the caution sounded out so clearly in Romans 14:1-4! She even maintained that killing animals, gave men the appetite for killing human beings, and therefore lies at the root of all warfare and murder.

The issue was highlighted at one of the CFO camps she attended. When asked why she ate only fruit, vegetables and bread, she shared her opinions, and faced 'quiet but strong disapproval'. Thereafter all further opportunities to speak at CFO camps came to an end, and after more than three years of happy fellowship at Glenn Clark's camps, Hannah found a further door closed behind her. So she made her way back to Hill House in England. 'What a God-inspired blessing my father gave me in such a faithful, kind friend as my stepmother,' she wrote in *Thou Shalt Remember* (p 121).

But such humble appreciation did not stop her trying to persuade Marjorie (unsuccessfully) to become a vegetarian too, and she could be quite demanding when it came to the kind of meals she expected Marjorie to prepare for her! She was also most insistent that Marjorie should never kill any angry wasp there might be in the room. Hannah believed that any pain inflicted on any animal, however tiny, was a pain inflicted on the Creator Himself.

III

In that same year, 1960, Rev. Ronald Adeney, who had sheltered with Ruth and Hannah in the grounds of CMJ's Hospital during the siege of Jerusalem in 1948, was appointed the first Warden of Stella Carmel, CMJ's newly acquired centre, a few miles east of Haifa. Nowadays, this former Arab millionaire's residence, is used as a Conference Centre for both Jewish and Arab believers, as well as being a well-appointed holiday hostel for tourists, and the base for a growing Messianic congregation.

Then in 1963, Hannah's friend, Ruth Clark, was awarded the MBE in the Queen's New Year's Honours List. She had served in the ranks of CMJ with distinction for fifty-three years, including that heroic period when she headed up the Girls School in war-torn Jerusalem.

Meanwhile, Hannah divided her time between a cottage near Tiberias in Israel, and her mobile home at Mersea. When more and more children began arriving on the island for their summer holidays, thus disturbing the quietness of this rather self-contained community, she seized the opportunity to invite some of them into her caravan, where they sang lots of lively new choruses, accompanied by a variety of ad hoc musical instruments. Then she told them spell-binding stories about the birds, crabs, oysters, and jellyfish they found along the shore! When she returned to Tiberias for the winter, she entertained the children of the Christian workers there with the same imaginative yarns, describing how sea creatures, animals and insects think about all the grown-up human beings who hover over them so menacingly.

As time went by, Hannah became a complete vegan, hating all modern farming methods, and refusing to eat any meat, eggs, or dairy produce. She wanted to live 'A Garden of Eden Lifestyle'. But fortunately, she was never totally logical about the idea – at least, while she never wore anything made of leather or wool, she did not give up wearing clothes altogether!

In the early days of her pilgrimage, she had discussed ideas with her father, Samuel, and his wisdom, patience, and quiet authority, would often save her from indulging her rampant imagination and more unrealistic opinions. But as he had died in 1949, and she had shut the door on evangelical life in 1956, there was little to curb her free spirit. In any case, throughout her career, she had never been a paid employee of any Christian organisation, so the normal disciplines Christian workers experience, did not apply to her.

IV

One day, Hannah received a newspaper cutting from America, which claimed that, according to some scientists,

plants and vegetables are also capable of feeling, since special testing devices had picked up what sounded like shrieks
of fear and anguish emitted by vegetables when they had
been thrown into hot water. Hannah was shocked by the
news. It left her nothing to eat at all!

At the time she was living in her mobile home, and she
'happened' to meet a market gardener at the communal
water tap the very next morning. So she asked his advice. To
her relief, he pointed out that when fruit has ripened, the
trees and bushes are glad to be relieved of it. In fact, if the
fruit is not picked, it is automatically shed. Presumably the
same was true of plants and vegetables as well.

But it never occurred to Hannah that sheep might likewise
be glad to get rid of their heavy woollen coats once the hot
weather arrived, and that there was therefore nothing wrong
in her wearing a woollen cardigan on a cold winter's day!
Nor did she consider how the explanation he had given could
give any comfort to shrieking vegetables when they got into
hot water!

Eventually, after becoming a vegetarian in 1960, and a
vegan in 1967, Hannah became a fruitarian in 1975, even
using the juice of almonds as a substitute for milk. She maintained that fruit juices removed harmful acids from the body,
and that arthritis and cancer cannot survive in one nourished
only on fresh fruits. She also taught that no harm ever comes
to 'the harmless one'.

But on her own admission, her weight dropped from ten to
seven-and-a-half stones, and at first, she lost her hair. Then
in the early 80s, she fell seriously ill while living in her house
above Tiberias, and had to be invalided home.

Marjorie arranged for her Pastor, Rev. Maurice Richards,
and a Red Cross nurse to meet Hannah at Heathrow Airport,
and to bring her back to Hill House for two weeks while she
recovered. There was some muddle over the time and
Terminal fixed for the arrival of Hannah's plane, and Rev.
Richards had to make for the Enquiry Desk. 'We don't know
of any plane from Israel at this time,' the young lady said in

reply to his enquiry, 'but there is a lady in a wheelchair around the corner. Perhaps she is the person you are looking for.'

Sure enough, there was Hannah, holding court from her invalid chair, looking extremely fragile, but surrounded by a group of stewards, medical staff and passengers, all listening to her thanking God with a joyful heart for all He had done for her. She seemed totally oblivious to all the confusion and kerfuffle around her. Hannah had long since learned to give thanks at *all* times.

She did not approve of orthodox medicine at this stage. But an Indian doctor was located at Witham, some twelve miles from Hill House, and he treated Hannah with acupuncture. Her condition was really quite serious. It seems that by eating only fruit, her body had become full of acid. So the doctor showed her how to make good use of lentils and rice to supplement her diet of fruit, and she slowly recovered, though not before her two weeks of convalescence had stretched into seven! It was really all quite a relief once the delightfully imperious Miss Hannah Hurnard was at last fit enough to be driven to her home on Mersea Island some ten miles away!

V

The final years of Hannah's life were spent in the companionship of her dear friend, Mrs Bernadette Fletcher. At first their summers were spent in Massachusetts, and the winters in Florida. But towards the end, they lived permanently on Marco Island off the west coast of Florida.

Eventually, Hannah was diagnosed as suffering from cancer of the colon, and was required to have surgery. But it is typical of Hannah's humility and honesty, that she should say in a letter to me on 12th November, 1989, shortly after the operation, and less than six months before she died,

I have been learning to appreciate the medical help given by doctors and nurses who sincerely long to relieve suffering human beings, even though their methods and remedies seem so unlike those practised and taught by the Lord Jesus. I have come to understand that *the older we grow, the more perfectly we need to practise all the Kingdom of Heaven teachings of the Lord Jesus*, if we want to maintain bodily health and strength. A tumor surgically removed from the bowels has challenged me to see that I was indeed again failing to show *bowels of mercy and kindness* to others who seemed to be acting in completely negative ways, just the opposite of those I believe in and write about. (See Phil 2:1, KJV.)

Each day, until near the end, Hannah would devote herself to study and writing. She would also enjoy her daily strolls along the beach. A Jewish lady living on the Island, recognised Hannah from years before when they had met in Israel. A professor who was in spiritual need, fell into conversation with her on the sands one day, and his life was turned round. People still gathered uninvited for Hannah's 'Ulpans'. Lives continued to be touched for good through her teaching.

But by the end of April 1990, it was clear that she was unlikely to live until her eighty-fifth birthday. She woke in the early hours of May 4th, and sang a chorus from years gone by:

There'll be no sorrow there,
In my Father's House, In my Father's House,
There'll be joy...joy...joy.

Then just before 3.40 a.m. she died as peacefully as she had lived for long years past. Her body was laid to rest in St Mary's Cemetery in Tewksbury, Massachusetts, by the loving care of her friend, Bernie Fletcher. On November 3rd, 1990, a Memorial Service was held for her on Marco Island, Florida.

The elaborate headstone which marks Hannah's final resting place, is quite unlike those simple stones that stand side by side over the Hurnard graves in the Quaker Burial Ground alongside Colchester's Roman Wall.

But while her earthly remains lie so far away from her roots in England and her home in Galilee, Hannah's friends and family rejoice to know that her present joy is to see the King in His beauty, in a land of far distances (Isa 33:17, KJV margin).

VI

Hannah has left behind the memory of a life that was touched by grace in a radical way.

Who could have believed that this morose, introspective, hateful youngster would blossom into such an outgoing, radiant witness for Christ? The helpless stutterer became a sparkling speaker. The girl who was so oppressed by fear that she could not bear to be in a locked room, not even a toilet (to her acute embarrassment), braved the guns of snipers in Galilee and the horrors of war in Jerusalem. The unbelieving and surly rebel was destined to be a prolific writer of faith-building books.

Here was a remarkable woman from a remarkable family. Her sister Ruth qualified as a doctor, and married the man who had prepared her for Confirmation: William Nathaniel Carter, an honoured member of staff at CMJ. Brother Bracy became a successful business man as his grandfather had been. While Naomi, the youngest of the family, lectured in history at Lady Margaret Hall, Oxford University, where she was a Don.

Hannah herself was from first to last an evangelist who had been bathed with a pentecost of God's love, first at Keswick in 1924, then more fully on Mount Olympus in 1950. To the end of her days, she sought the lost sheep of the House of Israel. But she had a heart enlarged by love to yearn over the whole sinning world of mankind.

FEB gave Hannah the vision and the method she needed for reaching out to both Jews and Arabs in the Holy Land, and for inspiring others to share her great adventure. She did not only discuss evangelism: she *did* it.

Hannah was a flawed genius. But she walked with God. The central reality of her religion was a love relationship with the Lord Jesus Christ. Whether expressing the romance of this relationship in spritely, charming verse, or summarising the blessings of discipleship in hymn-like poetry, Hannah's pilgrimage was marked by 'the beauty of holiness'. She has left behind the fragrance of a lovely life.

VII

Hannah has also bequeathed to us a clutch of splendid books which will continue to delight and inspire whole generations of readers, long after those who knew and loved her have departed this world.

Not all of her books deserve to be mentioned in the same breath. But Tyndale House Publishers in America, have judiciously selected those trustworthy titles of enduring worth. Some of these books have been highlighted here, notably *The Hearing Heart*, *Wayfarer in the Land*, *Watchman on the Walls* and *Hinds' Feet on High Places*. But there are others from her most creative period during the fifties, which are sure to have an on-going ministry.

She had a number of different writing styles. On the one hand, she wrote out of her heart about personal experiences. If her later books tended to become 'propaganda' rather than witness, her earlier works bear eloquent testimony to her ability to articulate the workings of grace in the secret places of her inner being. Like Bunyan, she charted the anatomy of the soul with unerring accuracy.

She was also capable of the most imaginative story-telling, producing at least three splendid allegories, laced with graceful poetry. *Hinds' Feet* is a classic. But if its sequel *Mountains of Spices* never quite captures the same rich quality, it is nevertheless a vivid portrayal of those Christian spices listed in Galatians 5:22,23, and shows how such spiritual fruit can entice others to 'taste and see that the Lord is good'.

As those extracts from her letters used in this memoire clearly show, Hannah was a wonderfully *descriptive* writer, with an eye for detail, a love for nature, an admiration for colleagues, and an instinct for a good story!

All these qualities, and more beside, come out of her journalistic books like *Wayfarer in the Land* and *Watchman on the Walls*. They are also seen to good effect in the half-yearly booklets she sent out to friends, as well as in those books of 'dialogue' which she wrote at an earlier stage: *The Secrets of the Kingdom* and *The Keys of the Kingdom*.

Hers was a questing nature. She was always hungry for more of God. And she wanted her fellow Christians to enjoy 'the Winged Life' for themselves. Her little book, *Walking among the Unseen*, contains many valuable extracts from this rich vein of devotional writing, and includes her memorable studies on the beatitudes. Her wonderful Testament, *The Kingdom of Love*, charts the way to holiness in a practical, pertinent and persuasive way.

One of her favourite texts in the Old Testament tells how corn is crushed so that bread can be baked (Isa 28:28,29). In fact she referred to the two books she wrote in 1950 as 'bruised corn', pounded to flour to make bread for others. Her half-yearly Ulpan books, were also described by her as 'loaf' booklets!

Hannah drew comfort from the fact that the 'threshing' described in those two verses, never lasts too long. God does not grind us into the ground. Instead, He works on us until such a time as He can see that we are ready to benefit from all His disciplines.

In such a way, Hannah discovered that while God had 'threshed' her life with all kinds of testing experiences, both as a girl at Hill House, and as a mature Christian worker in Israel, her task was to take the raw material of all such bruising, and turn it into written material that would encourage and bless her readers.

It was a calling she pursued with consummate skill and abiding effectiveness.

Acknowledged
with Gratitude

A s with all votes of thanks, someone is sure to get missed from this list! So my apologies in advance. But clearly I owe a great debt to Isabel Anders, Hannah's American biographer. She has inspired me to continue researching Hannah's story.

Marjorie Hurnard has been my main resource from day one. What a fine, upstanding, and gracious Christian she is! No wonder Hannah loved her dearly. It is sad that she has now lost her sight. But she remains as perceptive as ever.

Hugh Hurnard Carter has helped with the family tree, as also with snippets about the family, including his own father, Rev. William Nathaniel Carter, Hannah's brother-in-law.

Mrs Bernadette Fletcher kindly let me have the photo of Hannah used in this book. Rev. Maurice Richards, Hannah's former Pastor, and Rev. Rob Richards formerly of CMJ (no relation) have assisted, the former with reminiscences, the latter with access to CMJ's archives. Daphne English, the cook at Hill House, whom Samuel led to the Lord, and Peter Taylor, one of the gardeners, together with his wife Betty, have also shared treasured memories of Hannah with me.

Colchester Central Library, the Evangelical Library in London, and Zurich's Zentral Bibliothek, have been unfailingly helpful.

Hannah wrote three autobiographies. I've used CMJ's Fifth edition of *The Hearing Heart*. *The Opened Understanding*, her second autobiography, was published privately in 1958 and lodged in CMJ's archives. *Thou Shalt Remember*, written when

Hannah was eighty, and published by Harper & Row in 1988, is sadly out of print already.

The 1989 reprint of *Hinds' Feet on High Places* (Tyndale House Publishers) has been used here, as well as the Second edition of *Watchman on the Walls*, published by CMJ in July 1950. Hannah's struggle to come to terms with her father's remarriage, is told more fully in Chapter 5 of Hannah's guide to the more excellent way: *The Kingdom of Love* (pp 52-56 in Fourth edition, Olive Press, 1969). *Walking among the Unseen* was at one time published in the UK under the title *Simply by Faith*.

The discovery of so many extracts from Hannah's letters was very exciting. I had no idea that Marjorie's bound copies of the *Friends Witness*, which her late husband Samuel had co-edited, contained such treasures. Stanley L. Hunt of Northamptonshire have allowed me to use them at will.

Hannah's memory was not infallible. Whose is? I suspect that the Young Peoples' Meeting she attended at Keswick in 1924, may have taken place earlier in the week. Certainly the crucial prayer meeting which launched her village work in the Holy Land was in April 1937, and not in 1936 as she consistently said. Also, news of her father's death came six months *after* the first mailing she received from England following the War of Independence (contra p 119 in *Thou Shalt Remember*).

Some historical allusions used here, owe much to Longman's *Chronicle of the 20th Century* (1988), as well as to numerous books about Israel written in recent years. Information about FEB comes, not only from my own experience, but also from Mrs Bessie Bryers and her wonderful little book *To Them That Obey*, published by FEBV in 1969. Bessie also gleaned reminiscences of Hannah from Suzette Poole (née Clarke). Ruth Laurence, 'Sister Faith', went to her reward on May 6th, 1994, aged ninety-one.

There is no doubt that Hannah's theological shift caused very much pain within CMJ. But by then her work with the Society had run its course, and by now the memories have mellowed. Among folks in East Anglia, who knew her well, there are wry smiles about her sundry eccentricities! But while they remain bemused by her departure from that very evangelicalism which had motivated her life and ministry up to that point, they retain enormous respect for her. They knew her as one who lived in God's summerland of love.

Others better qualified than I will need to write about her later work in America. My concern has been to sketch the landscape of her pilgrimage from girlhood in Colchester to maturity in the Holy Land. That scenery has changed, of course. Hill House is in secular hands, the Temperance Hotel in Lexden is a block of apartments, Keswick is no longer the dominant force in evangelicalism which it once was, and the 'Palestine' Hannah knew and loved has developed tremendously in recent years. But the story of God's grace in her life remains an inspiration.

If Keswick 1951 was Hannah's swan song, so far as evangelicalism is concerned, it was in fact my overture. I'm now blessed to serve in the ranks of CMJ, to cherish so many of the splendid books Hannah wrote, and to share the story of a life that was touched by greatness. The name of Hannah Hurnard deserves to live long in our affections.

Landmarks in Hannah's Story

1571 The Hurnards and other Huguenots arrive in Colchester.

1572 Massacre of Huguenots on mainland Europe 23rd August.

1800 Robert Hurnard (26) marries Hannah Clark (32) 7th October.

1808 James Hurnard born at Chelmsford, 15th March.

1819 Robert and family sail for America in April. Lucy dies.

1824 Return to England.

1828 Ann dies at Kelvedon on 7th February, aged 22.

1835 Robert's wife Hannah dies, 11th November.

1866 James' father Robert dies on 7th January, aged 91.

1867 On 15th August, James marries Louisa Bowman Smith.

1869 Lexden Quaker School opened. Rose Densham born 23rd October.

1870 *The Setting Sun* by James Hurnard published.
        Samuel Fennell born to James and Louisa 17th August.

1873 James and family move to Hill House, 21st June.

1880 James elected Alderman of Colchester Borough (November)

1881 James dies on 26th February, aged 72.

1884 Louisa dies on 20th April in her 51st year.

1885 Opening of Lexden Village Hall, endowed by Louisa.

1895 May: Samuel elected JP, Lexden and Winstree Justices.

1899 Samuel Hurnard and Rose Densham marry, 23rd October.

1902 Frederick Richardson dies, 28th April.

1903 Samuel donates & unveils Memorial to Colchester martyrs.

1905 Hannah Rose Hurnard born, 31st May.

1911 Marjorie Eady and her twin Florence born 30th November.

1919	Friends Evangelistic Band formed (now FEBV).
1922	Rose spends last holiday with family in Switzerland.
1923	19th May to 30th September, Hannah at Tochterinstitut in Horgen.
1924	Keswick Convention, 19th – 27th July.
	Hannah goes to Ridgelands Bible College in September.
1925	Rose Densham Hurnard dies, 15th June, aged 55.
1926	Hannah joins FEB.
1929	Samuel, Bracy and Hannah visit Syria and Palestine.
1930	Hannah becomes Deputation Secretary for FEB.
1931	She is accepted to serve with British Jews Society.
1932	Arrives at Haifa on 21st January.
1934	Marjorie Eady goes to Redcliffe Bible College.
1936	Samuel Hurnard and Marjorie Eady marry on 27th May.
1937	14th October: Hannah commences her village work in Palestine.
1939	Daphne English starts work at Hill House, 2nd September.
1943	Hannah leases house at Rafidya to train village workers.
1946	Peter Taylor becomes a gardener at Hill House.
1947	Hannah returns to England via Egypt. Becomes Housekeeper at CMJ's Hospital in Jerusalem. Arrives there in October.
	Hannah's brother Bracy emigrates to New Zealand.
1948	State of Israel established, 14th May.
1949	Samuel Fennell Hurnard dies 13th January. Hannah returns to England. Stays at Braunwald in May.
1950	January: CMJ publish *Watchman on the Walls*. Hannah writes *The Hearing Heart*. Her 'second conversion'.
1951	Speaks at Missionary Meeting, Keswick in July.
1952	Flies to New Zealand in Spring. *The Hearing Heart* published by CMJ in September.
1954	*The Kingdom of Love* and *God's Transmitters* published. *Hinds' Feet on High Places* and *Mountains of Spices* written at Braunwald, Switzerland, in August.
1955	CMJ published *Hinds' Feet* and *The Winged Life*.
1956	September: Newsletter sent out explaining her new views.
1957	*The Heavenly Powers* and *The Inner Man* written.
1958	Launch of Ulpan ministry in America. Writes *The Opened Understanding*, her second autobiography.
1959	CMJ publishes *The Secrets of the Kingdom*.

1960	Hannah becomes a vegetarian.
1961	Her sister Ruth dies on 6th June.
1963	Hannah's friend, Ruth Clark, becomes MBE.
1967	Marjorie leaves Hill House. Hannah becomes a vegan.
1968	Hannah starts writing her 'loaf' booklets.
1969	After sale of Book Room in Colchester, Hannah buys cottage on Mersea Island. 23rd October leaves for her cottage at Doar Na Porryah 'Illit near Tiberias.
1973	Sells cottage at Tiberias. Translates *Comfort Ye My People* into Hebrew and Arabic. Distributes copies throughout the land. Breaks femur in Jerusalem. England in April, America in June and July, Mersea Island in August, New Zealand in December.
1975	Hannah becomes a fruitarian.
1981	*Eagles Wings to the Higher Places* completes her trilogy.
1984	Invalided home from Tiberias, cared for at Hill House.
1986	Hannah's sister Naomi dies, 29th August.
1988	Harper & Row publish *Thou Shalt Remember*.
1990	Bracy dies on 14th February, Hannah on 4th May.

From the Hurnard Family Tree

Robert Hurnard
(b 1774 d 7.1.1866)
m Hannah Clark
(b 1768 d 11.11.1835)
7.10.1800

| Lucy (d 1822?) | William Clark (d 2.2.1838) | Ann (d aged 22, 7.2.1828 | James (b 15.3.1808 d 26.2.1881) |

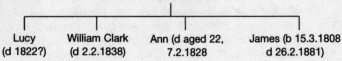

James (b 15.3.1808 d 26.2.1881)
m Louisa Bowman Smith (d 20.4.1884 aged 50)
15.8.1867

Samuel Fennell (b 17.8.1870 d 13.1.1949)
m Rose Densham (b 23.10.1869 d 15.6.1925)
23.10.1899

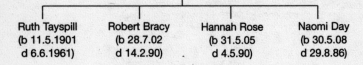

| Ruth Tayspill (b 11.5.1901 d 6.6.1961) | Robert Bracy (b 28.7.02 d 14.2.90) | Hannah Rose (b 31.5.05 d 4.5.90) | Naomi Day (b 30.5.08 d 29.8.86) |

Ruth Tayspill (b 11.5.01 d 6.6.61)
m William Nathaniel Carter (b 17.4.1881 d 3.4.69)
1927

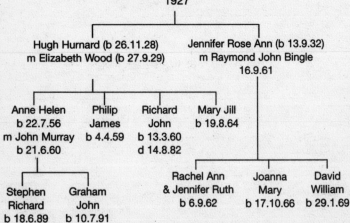

Hugh Hurnard (b 26.11.28)
m Elizabeth Wood (b 27.9.29)

Jennifer Rose Ann (b 13.9.32)
m Raymond John Bingle
16.9.61

| Anne Helen b 22.7.56 m John Murray b 21.6.60 | Philip James b 4.4.59 | Richard John b 13.3.60 d 14.8.82 | Mary Jill b 19.8.64 |

| Stephen Richard b 18.6.89 | Graham John b 10.7.91 |

| Rachel Ann & Jennifer Ruth b 6.9.62 | Joanna Mary b 17.10.66 | David William b 29.1.69 |

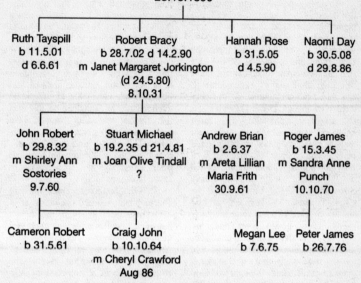

Samuel Fennell Hurnard
b 17.8.1870 d 13.1.1949
m Rose Densham
b 23.10.1869 d 15.6.1925
23.10.1899

Ruth Tayspill
b 11.5.01
d 6.6.61

Robert Bracy
b 28.7.02 d 14.2.90
m Janet Margaret Jorkington
(d 24.5.80)
8.10.31

Hannah Rose
b 31.5.05
d 4.5.90

Naomi Day
b 30.5.08
d 29.8.86

John Robert
b 29.8.32
m Shirley Ann
Sostories
9.7.60

Stuart Michael
b 19.2.35 d 21.4.81
m Joan Olive Tindall
?

Andrew Brian
b 2.6.37
m Areta Lillian
Maria Frith
30.9.61

Roger James
b 15.3.45
m Sandra Anne
Punch
10.10.70

Cameron Robert
b 31.5.61

Craig John
b 10.10.64
m Cheryl Crawford
Aug 86

Megan Lee
b 7.6.75

Peter James
b 26.7.76

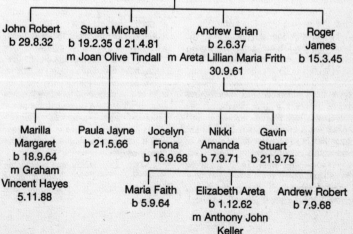

Robert Bracy Hurnard
b 28.7.02 d 14.2.90
m Janet Margaret Jorkington (d 24.5.80)
8.10.31

John Robert
b 29.8.32

Stuart Michael
b 19.2.35 d 21.4.81
m Joan Olive Tindall

Andrew Brian
b 2.6.37
m Areta Lillian Maria Frith
30.9.61

Roger
James
b 15.3.45

Marilla
Margaret
b 18.9.64
m Graham
Vincent Hayes
5.11.88

Paula Jayne
b 21.5.66

Jocelyn
Fiona
b 16.9.68

Nikki
Amanda
b 7.9.71

Gavin
Stuart
b 21.9.75

Maria Faith
b 5.9.64

Elizabeth Areta
b 1.12.62
m Anthony John
Keller

Andrew Robert
b 7.9.68

The Judgment of the Cross
By ROSE HURNARD.

So many people seem to ignore the fact of judgment altogether – pleading that God is too good and too kind to punish the creatures whom He has created – that it may be well to remind ourselves of the fact that a righteous God cannot look upon sin at all except to condemn it. Sin and holiness cannot, in the very nature of things, come into contact; the slightest shadow of evil must besmirch that which is pure and transparent. The proof that this needs be is in the Cross itself. He who is of purer eyes than to behold evil, turned away from our sinless, holy Substitute, as He hung upon the Cross, because God Himself had laid sin upon Him. If there were no judgment, there could have been no Calvary. The demands, the exactions of divine righteousness, holiness and justice were such that, if the sinner were to be justified, the heart of God must be wrung with anguish as He gave His only begotten One to meet the claims of His own divine nature. If judgment on sin be not a necessity, then our Lord Jesus Christ died as a martyr only.

One dare not, cannot speak of eternal judgment until one has cast one's soul back on the amazing fact that the eternal God has Himself suffered unutterable anguish, that the heart of the Divine Son was broken with the burden of sin which He bore in His own body on the tree, and that the demands of inexorable justice have been superbly and overwhelmingly settled in the death of the Saviour. God would not have forsaken Jesus upon the cross, would not have left Him to utter those words of indescribable entreaty – "My God, my God, why hast Thou forsaken Me?" had there been any other way. The greatness of the need stands proven by the greatness of the sacrifice which meets the need. The convicted prisoner in the dock, be he or she who they may, refined, cultured, tender-hearted, knows that no judge in any English Court dare declare them not guilty. He would be a judge no longer. He would dishonour his position, nay, he would dishonour his country. With man, it is an impossibility to clear the guilty, sentence must be passed, the demands of justice satisfied. God, that He might be what no human being can be, just and the justifier of guilty sinners, gave Jesus, and in giving Him, gave Himself, to meet and satisfy every claim of holiness and righteousness upon the guilty ones who believe in Jesus. (Romans iii.26.)

In Old Testament type, the fire completely consumed the sacrifice: in New Testament antitype, the victim consumed the fire of judgment. It was quenched for ever in eternal love, love which proved itself in righteousness. The glory of salvation is that the entrance of the redeemed soul into everlasting life and glory, does not depend upon the mercy, or the love, or even the power of God, but upon His righteousness. The Eternal One cannot justly keep one blood-bought soul out of the glory. He would deny Himself, His justice, by even the suggestion of such an action. You and I shall enter into His presence, not only as saved by grace, but on the ground of the righteousness of the holy God, who, in the Person of His Son, has met and settled forever the claims that might have brought us into judgment. Satan himself recognises the fact, for is he not a conquered foe? It is a question of identity. As sinner I am gone, crucified with Christ: as a sinner saved by grace, I have a new heart, and a new nature, and belong to the family of God.

NOTE. *This article was part of an open Paper read by the late Rose Hurnard several years ago, but not printed.*